AMERICA, DONALD TRUMP, GOD, and ME

THROUGH MY GREAT-GRANDMA EYES

TONI ME TAYLOR

ISBN 978-1-0980-6696-3 (paperback)
ISBN 978-1-0980-6697-0 (hardcover)
ISBN 978-1-0980-6698-7 (digital)

Christian Faith Publishing, Inc.
832 Park Avenue
Meadville, PA 16335
www.christianfaithpublishing.com

Printed in the United States of America

Dedicated to humanity

To every nationality, race, and ethnicity, for there is neither Jew nor Gentile, slave nor free, male or female. If we say we love God whom we have not seen but hate one another that we have seen, we are liars. We cannot love one and hate the other. We cannot hate one and love the other. It's all or nothing! A package deal! No picking! No choosing! No higher! No lower! No in-between! We are all one in the eyes of God. What we do and say to one another, we do and say to God. There's no separating God from His children. There's no separating God's children from their Father who is God.

We are God's creation, created conjointly, given dominion over the earth, endowed with the same liberties and freedoms. Yet there are those of us who believe we are better than others of us. Who are we to judge what we have neither the knowledge, wisdom, or understanding to know? God is Creator, Author, Maker, and Designer. He *alone* knows our causality—our who, what, when, where, and why. He *alone* knows the choices, mishaps, situations, conditions, and circumstances that shape and mold us. We see the visible things, the aftermath. God sees the invisible things, the hidden secrets of the heart, the cause resulting in the aftermath. He knows our entirety; our beginning, end, and everything in-between. He is the only One with the knowledge, wisdom, understanding, and authority to judge us justly. We are flawed; we harbor guilt, regret, and shame. None of us are just. None of us are good. None of us are more. None of us are less. None of us are worthy. Yet God says all of us are deserving. God is no respecter of persons; there is no partiality in Him. We are His children; there is no separating us. We are one in our Father's eyes. Who are we that we should see one another differently than our Father who is God?

IT TAKES COURAGE TO LOVE—*20 Letters*
Herein dwells opposition
Herein dwells Grace

IT TAKES NOTHING TO HATE—*20 Letters*
Herein dwells opportunity
Herein dwells Mercy

We are the body of Christ.
Glorious things dwell within us. Horrific things dwell within us.
We live in an unrighteous, dangerous world.
Yet amid unrighteousness, righteousness prevails.
Amid unrighteousness, God gave us hope.
Amid unrighteousness, God gave us—us…

Declaration of Evil

"Divide! Discredit! Distract! Destroy! Devour!"
Division of the races. Division of the sexes.
Division of personal preferences.
Division of religious beliefs. Division of political beliefs.
Divided you will *fail*! Divided you will *fall*!
I abide no race, no gender, no preference, no
religious belief; no political belief!
I abide self. I abide chaos.
I am barren. I am birthless. I cannot reproduce myself.
I cannot nourish myself.
I cannot multiply myself.
I cannot grow myself.
Hence, I cannot spread myself.
I need your power. I need your authority.
I need your minds, bodies, mouths, and limbs.
I need your permission.
Woe unto you!
For I am nothing without you!

Declaration of Good

God's will cannot change. It is fixed.
God's way changes constantly…
to give the spirit ample time to subdue the flesh.
God's grace and mercy keep human annihilation at bay.

*"The day of the Lord will come like a thief in
the night"* (1 Thessalonians 5:2).

On that day, God's will and God's way will be in one accord.
On that day, God's desire that none should perish gives way.
On that day, all shall be brought to bear.

Acknowledgments

My Creator and Father
God Jehovah
My Lord and Savior
Christ Jesus
My Comforter, Teacher, and Guide
Holy Spirit
Thank you, Lord Jesus, for doing for us what
we could not do for ourselves…
Save ourselves from ourselves

Special thanks to
Design illustrator Mark English

Apologies
To my family and friends who didn't know
about this book until now.

Faith is the substance of things hoped for the evidence of things not seen.
My Hope is in the Lord
He is my Sustenance. He is my Evidence. He
is my Confidence. He is my Strength.
Should I become lost in the obscurity of man,
let me be found in the Clarity of Christ.
To be ordinary in the eyes of the world
Is to be extraordinary in the eyes of Christ

SCRIPTURAL WORD OF KNOWLEDGE

To know the words of scripture yet not the
heart of scripture is to NOT know.
Knowing the words and the heart of scripture…
The Truth, the Way, and the Life
Eyes see. Spirit recognizes. Soul receives. Mind justly executes…
The Holy Scriptures
Knowing the words of scripture yet not the heart…
There is no Truth, there is no Life, there is, no Way, to rightly interpret
Eyes look but do not see. Spirit misinterprets. Soul
misrepresents. Mind unjustly executes…
The Holy Scriptures

Meaningful Beauty

The beauty of us resides in the whole of us. Though we are many; we are one. Jesus ransomed Himself that none might perish to bear on the beauty of us. Yet despite His sacrifice, some of us will most assuredly perish. Not by His hand but our own. How much of ourselves are we willing to ransom to bear on the beauty of us? How much of myself am I willing to ransom to bear on the beauty of you? If I do not answer "*all* of me," I am undeserving of Christ. I am undeserving of us. I am undeserving of you. I am undeserving of me. I am beautyless.

We are the beauty of Christ

We are God's love in motion

We are temples of the Holy Spirit

"Let us make man in our image, after our likeness."

****

Starting today and continuing forever

Let the beauty, love, and holiness of the One
dwelling within "us" be our legacy

Who Are You, America?

I am one nation under God indivisible. I am the Constitution of the United States. I am the Bill of Rights. I am the United States Declaration of Independence. I am We the People, every citizen, resident, foreigner, man, woman, and child. I am the rich, poor, and middle class. I am no respecter of person. I am the sword and scales of justice. I am the safe-keeper of freedom, liberty, and the pursuit of happiness. I am the guardian of freedoms, rights, privileges, immunities, articles, amendments, laws, and treaties, purpose-written herein; without regard to political affiliations, race, gender, or religious beliefs as set forth by my Founding Fathers. That all people, every race, color, and creed, living within my borders, visiting my shores, seeking asylum or refuge inside the safety my borders, be awarded equal freedoms, rights, liberties, privileges, and immunities. Let no citizen, resident, visitor, or those seeking refuge be treated inhumanely or unjustly.

I am past, present, and the yet to be determined future. I am the living, the dead, the born, aborted, and the yet to be born. I am every race, ethnicity, nationality, personal preference, religious belief, and disbelief. I am love restricted by hate, happiness crippled by despair, equality disavowed by inequality, truth distressed by lies, justice mocked by injustice, right deflated by wrong, good obstructed by bad, hope obscured by dread, compassion grieved by cruelty, comfort oppressed by misery, diversity shackled by uniformity, empathy derailed by apathy, joy haunted by atrocity.

There are those who prefer I disregard the indifference, hatred, death, pain, shame, misery, and sorrow from whence I come. What they prefer I cannot do. What they prefer, they cannot do; if they could, there would be no need for preference. I am multiculturalism at its best and its worst. I am generations past, generations present, and generations still to come. I am the constantly growing cumulative sum of those and that upon which I stand *thus far.*

I once was past. Land not lost yet supposedly found, claimed and inevitably stolen from a trusting, proud, unassuming people. Conquered by deceit, betrayal, covertness, greed, and lies. My original inhabitants slaughtered, shattered, scattered, and herded onto makeshift reservations constructed atop scorched earth. My blood-infused soil thrived at the hands of the beaten and broken, both native and foreign. Men, women, and children taken from distant lands, chained and imprisoned inside the bellies of tall sailing ships wherein women and young girls were often raped and impregnated by husbands and men not their own. Branded livestock sold and traded at auction in exchange for currency and material goods. Hundreds of years have passed since my misappropriation and colonization. Many things have changed since then; many other things remain the same. *I am beauty from tragedy, ash, blood, and bone.*

I am now present. Abundant for some, meager for others. I am the impoverished pushed low, the wealthy held high, and the in-between neither low nor high. I am culpability in motion, the long-awaited victory for those presumed defeated, the long-awaited defeat for those presumed victorious. I am waylaid justice, righteous indignation, retaliation, retribution, restoration, and liberation! I am the disquieting unified voices of the molested, abused, misused, discarded and conveniently forgotten. I am dark things brought to light, horrific truths exposed, heinous lies deposed.

Amid unrighteousness I become righteousness! Amid weakness I become strength! Amid fear I become fearless! Amid whisper I become roar! Amid blindness I become sight! Amid deafness I become sound! Amid brokenness I become whole! Amid secrecy I become revelation.

I await my future. The alliance of nations, one people under God indivisible; dedicated to the freedom, equality, liberty, justice, preservation, and enrichment of *all* humankind. Abundant for all! Meager for none! Outstretched arms to everyone, clenched fist to no one. I am the raised voices, differing views, and opinions of the many. I am *not*—and hope never again shall be—the imprudent, self-serving, narrow-minded, whispering voices, views, and opinions of the few. I am *not* a singular belief, preference, or ideology. I am we the people! I am impartiality, the freedom to choose without detriment. I am learned knowledge awaiting the mastery of wisdom. I am! *E Pluribus Unum*, out of many, one. *I am everyone, lest I become no one.*

I am the United States of America! United I stand! Divided I fall! I pledge allegiance to the inclusive majority, having no allegiance to the divisive minority. I am a sanctuary. I am open waters. I am welcoming shores. I am resolute. I shall not waver. I shall not be moved. For those with eyes to see and ears to hear,

> Give me your tired, your poor, your huddled masses yearning to breathe free, The wretched refuse of your teeming shore. Send these, the homeless, tempest-tossed to me; I lift my lamp beside the golden door!

Let the past from whence I came not become my present. Let what was gained not become lost.

I Pledge Allegiance

"To the flag of the United States of America."

*"I pledge allegiance to the flag of the United States of America
and to the Republic for which it stands,
one nation, under God,
indivisible, with liberty and justice for all."*

*****

What do I see when I look at the American flag?
I see...

*The Stars in the Heavens
The Red, Innocent, Gallantly Streaming Blood of Christ Jesus*

The White, Impartial, Liberty, Freedom,
Love and Purity of God Jehovah
The Blue Purging Fires, Cleansing Waters,
Consoling Winds of the Holy Spirit
I see…
Sacrifice, Salvation, Absolution, Intercession,
Love, Forgiveness, Grace, and Mercy…
Father, Son, Holy Ghost

*****

To these three divine, impartial colors, I pledge my allegiance.
Which begs the question

Why is it, we beam with delight, in the presence of the life-less, red, white, and blue, stars and stripes, cotton manufactured, flag colors, created by man; yet scowl with contempt, in the presence of the living, breathing human colors; created by God, for which the American flag "supposedly" stands and waves? The emblem of the American flag; *"Liberty, freedom, and justice for all"*. The motto of the United States of America; *"In God we trust."*

Like it or not, for better or worse; we are reflections of one another. Knowing this to be true; gives me pause: What do we see when we look at one another? What is it about some of us, that drives others of us to such hate-driven; intractable conflict—regarding skin color? Bearing in mind; we are "all" created in the image of God. According to Him, who is no respecter of persons, there is no sepa-ration of persons; hence there is no separation of skin color; hence there is no separation, of human rights, freedoms, or liberties. We are the children of God. We are the Body of Christ, appointed by our Creator to guard, protect, and be of service, to all therein. We are responsible for "our" sick and weary; "our" poor and hungry; "our" hurting and destitute; "our" abused and misused; "our" lost and for-saken; "our" rejected and disrespected; "our" bleeding and broken. We are—We the People! We are Not—we some of the people.

What man calls black, white, brown, yellow, red, male, and female; God calls beloved child. There will soon come a day, after all, is said and done, the last breath on earth is taken, human flesh dissolves into sinlessness, creature comforts crumble into dust, and this world ceases to exist. On that day, the Holy Spirit returns to the Kingdom of Heaven. On that day, we come full-circle, back to from whence we came. On that day, we stand naked and alone before the Lord. On that day, we will give a full accounting of our earthly existence. On that day we see in spirit; what we refused to see; in flesh— that there was no skin color, there was no male, there was no female, there was no higher, there was no lower, there was no better, there was no worse, there was no them; there was no they; there was only us—we the people. We the children of God, and the consequences of our choices. On that day, the sentence we lived on earth, the sentence we so ordered, by way of intent, consistent with our free will/choices; is examined, measured, weighed, judged, and implemented.

Nevertheless! Today! Right here! Right now! We have the power! We have the authority!—to effect change! We choose!—to be! We choose!—not to be! United in love! Or divided by hate! We—this present generation are; the multihued; multicultural foundation, upon which future generations will stand and build. As past generations gave birth to this present generation/our generation, so shall we/this present generation give birth to future generations. The choices we made yesterday, the choices we make today, the choices we make tomorrow will impact the choices of succeeding generations long after this present generation/our generation is dead and gone. What we do and say to some of us we do and say to all of us not only this present generation/our generation, but future generations. Inequality breeds injustice. Injustice breeds inequality. They are one, and the same. They cannot change. We, the people, can! There is no such thing as things will never get better. There is no such thing as things can't get any worse. We are our better! We are our worse! We decide where we go from here!

Gracefully Broken

The world broke me from the inside out. Having no further need of me, it gathered up my broken pieces, took me to an abandoned landfill, and threw me atop a garbage heap. One day God was passing overhead, looked down and took notice of me. I was disfigured by sin and covered in filth, yet He recognized me, and my stench did not offend Him. My brokenness was massive; countless shards of shame, loathing, fear, and desperation. God tilted His head to the side, smiled, and said, "I'm right here; I have not forsaken you."

My decomposing ears perked up, my broken heart skipped a beat, my cracked lips smiled, my sunken eyes filled with tears; my Lord had not forsaken me. God wiped my tears away with His right hand while sifting through the mound of rotting garbage encasing me with His left. Having found every piece of me, He called down the cleansing rains and gentle breeze of heaven. The warm cleansing rain soothed my rotted, tormented flesh and washed away my stench. The gentle breeze lifted me up and swirled my brokenness into place.

God smiled at me, wrapped me in grace and mercy, and hugged me whole. He did not say the world would be kinder. He did not say I would never feel shame, despair, fear, or never be broken again; only that He loves me. In Him I am found; in Him I am made new; in Him I am complete. But the world wasn't ready to let me go. It continued looking for new ways to break and old ways to rebreak. But I wasn't the person I used to be. I know who I am. I know what I am. I know why I am. I know who I belong to. The world thought it had me, but God, my God came and got me! He cleansed me from the inside out! He freed me! He graced me back to health! He made me whole! Yes, I still crack from time to time; occasionally, I even break! But I never shatter!

God loved me; He forgave me in spite of me, in spite of the life I chose to live, contrary to Him. He hid me beneath His wings. He taught me how to love and forgive myself, how to love and forgive my enemies, how to love, forgive, live, and let go. Let go of fear, anger, hurt, pain, and shame. God's love and forgiveness freed me—freed me to discern, spiritually, what I could not understand physically. That love and forgiveness are the reason for *everything*! Everything that was. Everything that is. Everything that is still to come. To love is to forgive; to forgive is to love—they are *inseparable*. God's love restored me. God's forgiveness renewed me. I surrendered to God's plan. At that moment, the world lost its hold on me. My need, want, and desire become one. God's peace envelops me, and I wake to find God was all I ever needed. That though I falter, though I fail, He does not.

And there came a second moment—a moment of absolute clarity. Love and forgiveness are the reasons God sent His Son to earth to suffer and die for us. Love and forgiveness are the reasons Christ allowed himself to be captured, persecuted, tortured, and crucified for us. Love and forgiveness are the reasons the Holy Spirit left the kingdom of heaven, came to earth, and remains to this day—to comfort, encourage, guide, and teach us. Love and forgiveness fulfill the precepts, statutes, ordinances, divine law, commands, rules, and the first law of God. Accepting the love and forgiveness of God the Father, the Son, and the Holy Spirit is a personal choice—*not a mandate of God.*

Introduction

My name is Toni Moses Esther Taylor. I was born on February 19, 1949, in Birmingham, Alabama. My biological father, John Henry Taylor, named me Toni. Mom would later tell me dad named me after a cartoon character he liked. On my fiftieth birthday, my Heavenly Father, God Jehovah, honored me with the name Moses Esther; a prophet and a queen. I am a Christian African American female. I have three children and ten grandchildren. I began writing this book on February 19, 2018, my sixty-ninth birthday. It was completed on my seventy-first birthday. At the start of this book, I had one great-grandchild; I now have four.

Before I tell you why I wrote this book, I'd like to share a few things about myself. I've been writing since I was eight years old. Growing up, reality was my enemy, imagination my only friend. That being said, never in a million years would I have imagined writing something like this. I'm more into whodunits, mysteries, fantasies, and science fiction. I wrote my first book ten years ago, a spiritual fantasy, 102,126 words, 406 pages, loaded with action, thrills and chills, warrior angels and diabolical demons. That book didn't take anywhere near as long to write as this little book. I couldn't wait to see it in print yet was never led to seek its publication. Now that I've written this, I understand why. To everything, there is a season and a time for every purpose under heaven; then was not the season nor the time—for my fantasy. For this little book, this is the time; this is the season—for my reality.

Though this book is titled *America, Donald Trump, God, and Me: Through My Great-Grandma Eyes*, the more I remember, write, and assimilate, the more I realize what I'm writing is more than the title implies—more than America, more than the president, more than me. As I look back over my life, I don't just see me; I see us. I see we! We the people! We *all* people! We the body of Christ! We the temples of the Holy Spirit! We the sons and daughters of God!

Though it is not good to dwell on the past, not forgetting past atrocities brings compassionate healing to the present, a hope, and a future. Minimizing past atrocities, denying the truth to mislead, hide, and booster the lies and wickedness of the present make way for the reemergence of past atrocities, therein constituting a viable threat to the present generation and future generations. Confronting the pending darkness, here and now, united and unafraid, hurries God's impending light.

We are God's lighthouses standing amid the world's raging storms! We pave, light, and secure the way! We are sword! We are shield! We hold the prime evils at bay. We are the safe-keepers, the guardians of future generations! We are, we the people! We God's people! United we stand! Divided we fall!

Though I was born in Birmingham, Alabama, I grew up in Detroit, Michigan. I am the second oldest of seven children, six girls and one boy. My mom, Walterine Cannon-Taylor, my dad, John Henry Taylor, three of my sisters and my brother are now deceased. Some of what you're about to read about me is good, some not so good. This is who I was, this is who I am, but more importantly, this is who I am not—I am not this worldly place. My flesh is temporary; my spirit eternal; my citizenship heaven. My place is with my Savior, Christ Jesus. It took me a minute to get from where I was to where I am, and by a minute, I mean years. Accepting the scared responsibility of free will as endowed by God—with all its grace and tender mercies and letting go of the disingenuous secular right and freedom to choose, as set down by man with all its pride and prejudices—was an easy choice to make once I had eyes to see and ears to hear God's one truth amid man's countless lies.

Free will as endowed by God is self-rule. Whether my choice is good, bad, right, wrong, or indifferent, my choice is mine in accordance with my will—no one else's. The right and freedom to choose as promised by man yet dictated by the world required I yield in accordance with its will, societal whims, views, and opinions. I was at the most critical junction of my life; two paths lay before me. Surrender my life to God, allow Him to restore and implement the divine path/truth He designed me to follow. Walk His path, live His truth for the remainder of my life, and in-so-doing finally know what it means to live and not die. Or surrender my life to the world, continue down the path/lie of self-destruction Lucifer laid down for me as a child. Walk his path and live his lie for the remainder of my life and in-so-doing never know what it means to live and not die, only the eternal sorrow of living death.

I questioned everyone and everything in my life when I was young, scrutinized every coincidence and happenstance, always searching for why always looking for a way out or around all the bad in my life. I've grown a lot older and a lot wiser since then, old enough and wise enough to know there's no such thing as coincidence or happenstance; and more oftentimes than not, there is no way around, there is no way out; only through. Everything in my life that happened or is currently happening happened or is happening for a specific reason; nothing in my life is random. Nothing happens unless God allows. Everything God allows, He allows to reveal and/or teach me something about me, others, or a situation.

Where I'm headed, God has already been, subsequently, what He allows, He allows based on what only He knows, with consideration to what I thought I knew, what I think I know, and what I have yet to know. God allows based on choices I've made, choices I'm currently making, choices I have yet to make but surely will, as well as choices made by others that adversely affect me; be those choices intentional or unintentional. That being said, God permits what I permit. God binds what I bind. What I lose, God allows to be loosed in accordance with my free will.

What you hold in your hands is my testimony; my graceful brokenness; my past, present, and in-between—a past painfully resurrected, an in-between sorrowfully remembered, a present reflection of both my past and in-between. I pray, sharing *all* of me, the good and not so good helps us become a kinder, gentler, more considerate, respectful people. There is no mention of them or they amid these pages. There is no them; there is no they, only us! We the people! We God's people!

Hopefully, sharing these things about myself will offer some degree of solace. I'm not some angry black woman with a chip on her shoulder, feebleminded senior citizen with too much time on her hands, or religious zealot out to convert the world. I do, however, confess I love God and all created by Him with all that I am. Having confessed that, I must also confess this: I haven't always felt this way. There was a time when I wanted nothing to do with God, His Son, His Holy Spirit, or His people. My only exception being immediate family, primarily my children, and a sparse number of friends whom, if I'm being honest, also found difficult to tolerate from time to time. I was in my midforties when I finally embraced God. Embracing humans took a bit longer.

I couldn't understand why we humans put so much time and effort into hurting one another yet so little time and effort into helping one another. Equally ununderstandable to me was the joy some of us appeared to get from hurting others. The harder I tried to trust us, the more I distrusted us. The more sense I tried to make of us, the less sense we made. I ultimately decide to keep my distance from every one except immediate family and those few sparse friends.

On my fifth birthday, right after He changed my name, God invited me to become a messenger of service. He and I were in such a good place I accepted with no hesitation. I trusted God so much, whatever He wanted me to do is what I wanted to do. For the first time in my life, I started to trust myself, trust that with God, anything is possible. But when it came to letting my guard down and trusting people, I just couldn't. We, humans, are so unpredictable; there's no way of knowing what we're going to do or say. What if I deliver God's message and nothing changes? What if people don't believe me? What if people think I'm crazy? What if, what if, what if. I want to please God. I want to be of service to others. How can I do that when I'm too afraid to trust? I suddenly realize, despite how much I want to please God, I still have a long way to go and grow heart, mind, soul, and spirit.

When the heart, mind, soul, and spirit collaborate, when they grow in knowledge and wisdom conjointly, mountains become mole hills; cold, troubled waters become warm, calming streams; raging storms become gentle rains; howling winds become tender breezes; crooked roads are made straight; and darkness makes way for light. Spiritual maturity weathers the trials and tribulation of physical immaturity, makes painful things bearable, complicated things less complicated, and the unforgivable things forgivable. The spirit endures when the soul cannot.

As I grew in the fullness of Christ, I grew in the fullness of me. It took me fifty years to accept I am solely responsible for myself. That I can be an example to others, but the only person I can change is me. I can't change what people say, think, or how they feel about me, but what I can change is how I allow their words and actions to affect me. There are no prerequisites to serve or be of service. I didn't need to trust others to be of service; I only needed to trust God. As long as I trust God, everyone and everything will fall into place. To be of service to God is to be of service to His people; to be of service to His people is to be of service to him. One can't be serviced without servicing the other. To truly be of service is to serve expecting nothing in return. It is expected—regardless of the wrongs done to me—I will do no wrong in return. I share these things that you might understand how I got from where I was to where I am—my truth, want, hope, and desire.

My life truth. God Jehovah is my Father, Author, Maker, Designer, and Creator. Christ Jesus is my Lord, Redeemer, and Savior. The Holy Spirit is my Comforter, Teacher, and Guide. I am a member of the body of Christ. Though I am one, I am many. Regardless of malicious deeds, ill-spoken words, or harsh circumstances, I will do *no* harm to the body of Christ.

My unquestioning truth. We are God's children created in His image and likeness and conjointly given dominion over the rest of creation. We were created a loving, kind, thoughtful, compassionate, empathetic, purposeful people. Though we are many, we are one. Each of us designed in anticipation with consideration of the other. No one of us deemed higher or lower than the other. No one of us deemed more or less than the other.

God knew who and what we would become eons before He created us. He knew our carnal nature; our capacity for sin. He knew the grief, hurt, pain, misery, death, devastation, and destruction we would cause; the lies we would tell; and the atrocities we would commit. He knew, regardless of how much He loved us, our sin nature would override His love. He knew one day, in order to save us, He would sacrifice His Son. He knew these things to be absolute, He knew these absolutes would not change because we would not change. Yet generation after generation, He deems us deserving. Generation after generation, He takes the best and worse parts of us into His thoughtful consideration. Generation after generation, Christ Jesus intercedes on our behalf. Generation after generation, the Holy Spirit "mans" His post within.

Knowing this unquestioning truth bolsters my confidence and continually renews my faith, though seemingly microscopic; moral excellence dwells within us. That moral excellence notwithstanding its small measure reassures me time and time again God has not forsaken us. Knowing this unquestioning truth helped me rediscover my spirituality; my who, what, and why. Knowing who, what, and why I am, spiritually, quiets my flesh, calms my mind, comforts my soul, and soothes my heart even during the most troubling of times.

My questioning truth. If we no longer consider ourselves children of God; if we do not consider ourselves joint-heirs; if we liken ourselves to the world more so than our Creator; if we no longer acknowledge our original design; if we have forsaken God's law to become laws unto ourselves accountable only to ourselves; if we prefer division over unity; if we consider some of us lesser than others of us; if we believe a person's significance resides in skin color, national origin, social status, wealth or the lack thereof; if we no longer have an allegiance with God; if we are no longer a loving, kind, thoughtful, compassionate, empathetic, purposeful people; if we prefer evolution over creation, who are we? What are we? Why are we? If we no longer bear God's image and likeness, whose image and likeness do we bear? Whose purpose do we serve? To whom/what do we pledge our allegiance? In whom/what do we abide? In whom/what do we believe?

My sorrowful truth. We abide lies in lieu of truth, yet the lies we tell do not excuse nor lessen the pain and suffering we cause. Lies merely provide the justification we need to live with our lies. Lies are traffickers of death; they are evil's nourishment. Every facet of evil is rooted in the manure of our lies. Evil delights in our arrogance, prejudices, self-proclaimed righteousness, hypocrisy, and degradation. Not because of the pain we cause one another but because of the pain we cause God. God is primary, we're secondary. We are the means to evil's end.

Every evil thing we do and say against one another, we do and say against ourselves and God. Our ill-spoken words and misdeeds sustain evil's hold on us, Our wrongdoings are its sustenance. Evil would have us believe our wrongdoing is justified, that sometimes doing wrong is right when it comes to protecting ourselves, our family, and our livelihood. Thing is, there is no justifying wrong. Wrong always returns to, from whence it came, oftentimes attacking the very persons and/or things we lied to protect. Evil cannot be justified or satisfied. Its belly cannot be filled, its thirst cannot be quenched; the more pain, hurt, and misery we cause, the more, evil craves. We don't do what evil allows; evil does what we allow. We are the deciding factor. We allowed hate and lies to divide us. That division has given evil access to power we can't begin to understand. Evil is plowing his way through America, and establishing strongholds along the way. He ain't letting up! He ain't slowing down! He sure as heck ain't stopping! Why would he?! This present generation/our generation is the closest he's come to annihilating mankind—in centuries! Love and Unity are our greatest strength and defense. United by love, we weaken evils' power and slow his plans. Division and hate are evil's greatest strength and offense. Divided by hate; we increase evil's power and accelerate his plan. Evil is using us to destroy us.

Evil can't spread amid truth and unity. Truth can't spread amid lies and division. Truth is life! Lies are death! United in truth, we stop evil! Divided by lies evil stops us! So why now? Why is evil so hell-bent on destroying America in this present generation/our generation? Short answer: *Risk Management Control Assessment.* Evil knows, if he doesn't spiritually bankrupt this present generation/our generation; before we become fully aware before we stop looking and start seeing before we stop hearing and start listening it's only a matter of time before we/this present generation, stop "allowing" ourselves to be deceived, and lied to. He knows, when that time comes, we will "see" our United Truth! We will hear our United Voice! We will "perceive" our United Strength Durability! Evil knows, if that happens, there'll be no stopping us!— We will be United in Solidarity! We will "know" our Who, What, and Why! Who we are!—*the safe-keepers of life, liberty, and the pursuit of happiness!* What we are—*the protectors of justice and inalienable rights!* Why we are—*the guardians of freedom and equality!*

The choices we make in this present generation; will either empower or enslave the coming generations. It falls to us/this present generation to restore America's hope for a future. It falls to us/this present generation to secure the foundation upon which future generations will stand and build. It falls to us/this present generation to rebuild what we wrecked; that recompense of our greed, arrogance, indifference, and selfishness, not fall, to future generations. We are the Body of Christ! Authored, designed, selected, and fully-equipped by God, our Creator to protect, guard, and defend "all" humankind. For us to do less; is for us to be less! Less than God created us to be. Less than Christ lived, was crucified and died for us to be. Less than the Holy Spirit left the Kingdom of Heaven to reside on earth, for us to be. Less than; We the people deserve us to be.

My want—that whoever sees and hears me, sees and hears Christ in me.

My hope—that my life on earth added value to God's hope for mankind.

My desire—that humankind restores itself to God's original design.

Growing Up Toni Taylor

Growing up Toni Taylor is more than a notion. My dad works manual labor jobs from time to time but fancies himself a pimp. Momma calls Daddy a rolling-stone wannabe pimp yet caters to his every whim. I have two siblings, an older sister and a younger brother. It's rumored Momma isn't the only woman in Daddy's life, that he has a lot more women and a lot more kids, but no one knows for sure how many. Be that as it may, my mom is the woman Daddy chose to marry.

Mom is a mother and housewife. Her family is her world. Pleasing daddy, taking care of us kids and keeping a spotless house is her heart, pride, and joy. Mom knows what Daddy's up to when he's out roaming the streets. She even confronts him about his philandering from time to time, but Daddy knows Mom just as well as she knows him. He knows, no matter how much Momma complains, she loves him and isn't going anywhere. Then one day, out of the blue, Daddy decides he doesn't want to be a husband or a father anymore; he wants to be a full-time pimp. It takes a while, but Momma finally accepts her painful truth; her marriage is over. Neither Mom nor Dad filed for divorce when they died; they were still married.

A year or so after Mom and Dad call it quits, she meets and falls in love with someone else. He isn't Daddy, but he makes her laugh. Their relationship lasts less than a year, and our family increases by one, a baby girl. A couple of years later, Mom falls in love again; she says he's our "stepfather" and allows him to move in with us. He's a hustler like my dad but also works at Great Lakes Steel. He buys Mom lots of nice things, makes sure the bills are paid, and there's always plenty of food in the fridge. He and Mom seem happy. They have a lot of mutual friends; our house is the weekend place to be. Several years and three daughters later, Mom and the stepfather call it quits. Mom is on her own again; our family of five is now eight.

Mom's a proud woman. She hates asking anyone for help. Thankfully, she cares more about her kids than her pride. She goes to each of our dads and asks for help. They hem and haw but finally agree to do what they can. Sadly, they're what they can, lasts around three months. As far as outward appearance, likes, dislikes, employment, or the lack thereof goes, our dads have nothing in common; but when it comes to deadbeat dads, they're exactly the same. I never understood why Mom didn't take their sorry behinds to court. I learn early on, love practiced and love spoken aren't the same; promises made are easier broken than promises kept, good, bad, or indifferent; actions speak louder than words.

Momma can do most anything she puts her mind to—hairdressing, sewing, arts and crafts, plumbing, masonry, electrical work; she's pretty much a female jack of all trades, not to mention an incredible cook. Yet despite all she knows, she can't find a decent job. She lacks what employers call employable skills. Mom does everything she can to keep us afloat—cooking, cleaning, sewing, washing, ironing; taking care of other folks' kids, but no matter how much she does or how hard she works, she makes barely enough money to make ends meet.

It's only after our lights and gas are disconnected for the umpteenth time, Mom having to put cardboard in the soles of our shoes to cover the holes, eating pinto beans two or three days in a row, then adding elbow macaroni to stretch them into five days, eating buttermilk and cornbread the remaining days of the week, sending us off to school with leftover, cold cow tongue, Miracle Whip sandwiches for lunch, kids making fun of us, and us coming home in tears that Mom finally applies for AFDC (Aid to Families with Dependent Children), which she swears we won't be on for more than a few months but turns into years.

Mom decides she needs to go back to school, but the chances of that happening are pretty much nil and none. There's eight of us now. Even with government assistance and Mom making money on the side, we're still scarcely getting by. But as luck/God would have it, the government doesn't want Mom on ADC any more than she wants to be on it. She enrolls in a state-sponsored job training program, graduates, and gets a clerical job working for the State of Michigan, where she works until her retirement.

Like many Americans, I grew up in the church, which at our house means 10:00 a.m. Sunday-morning service, 6:00 p.m. Sunday evening service, and Wednesday Bible Study. Sadly, all that "church," the pastor's constant wheezing hallelujas, let the church say amen sermons; wives decked out in their Sunday best look-at-me-attire draped on the arms of their sharkskin suit, parading, wandering-eyed husbands; and my do as I say, not as I do "religiously correct" grandma, don't teach me a single thing about what it means to be a Christian.

What I do learn at a young age; the church ain't what it pretends to be. Getting baptized, don't make you a Christian. Christians are hypocrites. The people in my family professing to Christians are even bigger hypocrites. Religious titles don't mean crap! Talking Jesus and living Jesus; ain't the same. Just because a house looks like a home, don't mean it is. Just because you think you know someone don't mean you do. Abuse of power and authority rapes the body, devastates the spirit, and breaks the soul. Familiar people go bump in the night. Monsters have familiar faces. Fear has familiar names. Corrupt adults, corrupt children. Dreams are nightmares pretending to be dreams. Tears don't have a purpose. People would rather believe a lie than confront the truth. Prayer doesn't work. Children are powerless. God loves everyone except me. Jesus saves everyone except me. The Holy Spirit lives inside everyone except me.

I hate being a kid, but I hate being a girl even more. All I do is cry. I despise church. I detest home, and I hate everybody. Are they all blind? Why, can't anyone see what's happening to me? Getting older is my only comfort, knowing one day I'll be old enough to escape the two places I hate most. The pretend place, my pretend family calls home, and the pretend place, pretend Christians call church. But I'm a child, so I reason like a child. I'm too young, too naïve, to understand, my hatred, bitterness, and shame are growing right along with me.

I'm well into my thirties before I fully accept, the house I grew up in, was never my home; family isn't defined by biology; worldly titles are subjective; looks can be deceiving; my spirit has my best interest at heart, my flesh is my enemy; trust should be earned, never given; when you look for wrong in others, wrong reveals itself in you; ill-intent breeds ill-intent; Christianity and religion are not the same thing; never make assumptions; tears heal the soul; prayer works; forgiveness begins within; God loves everyone, especially angry little girls. Jesus saves everyone, especially terrified little girls. The Holy Spirit lives inside everyone, even disbelieving little girls. In time, young hearts mature. Broken hearts mend. Hearts of stone become flesh. And through hearts' restored beat differently, Christ's heart song stays the same. Physical churches built by men are not—the Church! They are places of worship, sanctuaries, synagogues, temples, etcetera; built by mankind for mankind. Temporary, earth-bound buildings; constructed to house the assembled Body/Church of Christ.

"Now you are the body of Christ and individually members of it. And God has appointed in the church first apostles, second prophets, third teachers, then miracles, then gifts of healing, helping, administrating, and various kinds of tongues. Are all apostles? Are all prophets? Are all teachers? Do all work miracles? Do all possess gifts of healing? Do all speak with tongues? Do all interpret? But earnestly desire the higher gifts. And I will show you a still more excellent way." 1 Corinthians 12: 27–31

And last but not least, the unwelcoming, weather-beaten, single-story building I was forced to attend as a child twice on Sunday and every Wednesday isn't the church Jesus was referring to when He said, "Upon this rock, I will build My church." Matthews 6:18

All of these amazing things are revealed to me in the spirit, but I'm so broken, my hatred and anger run so deep it's not enough to hold me. Here today, gone tomorrow! Righteous on Sunday, sinful on Monday. Christ time, not my time. God's inconvenient truth today, the world's convenient come hither lies tomorrow. Take the narrow, least-traveled road of the few or the wide most-traveled road of the many. Here's the thing, I've been through a lot in my young life. I don't give a hoot about anyone or anything not beneficial to me. Yes, I'm stupid! But as I mentioned earlier, I'm young. You don't have to be a genius to figure out which road I took. I still have a long way to go and a long way to grow before I finally get it.

I have my first child at sixteen, marry at seventeen, have my second child at eighteen, my third child at twenty-one, miscarry at twenty-three, and divorce at twenty-four. I don't finish high school. My only job experience is working at the neighborhood confectionary. Other than being quite a bit younger than my mom was, and only having three kids to take care of instead of seven, my life was starting to look a lot like hers; something I swore my life would never be. I am so happy to get out of my mom's house; so happy not to hear her nagging voice; so happy not to follow her house rules; so happy to do what I wanted when I wanted; so happy to be grown and own my own. Stupid! Stupid! Stupid! I'm so nowhere near grown.

The only thing I did when I stomped out of my mother's house was jump out of the frying pan into the fire! Within a matter of months of "living grown" and on my own, life/my husband teaches me regardless of how old I get, regardless of how many babies I have, whether I'm single or married, I will always need my mother. No one will ever love me the way she does. Turns out, the man I "thought" I loved, married, and kicked my mom to the curb for, isn't the man he pretended to be or the man I imagined him to be. He's my biological father and the stepfather; he just looks different and answers to a different name. The house I'm living in, his house, is the same house I grew up in; it just looks different and has a different address. I'm right back where I started from. I don't know what's worse, being constantly told how worthless I am, or being periodically beaten into worthlessness. After years of abuse, I finally muster up enough courage to leave.

I squirrel away as much clothing for me and my kids as I can. We don't have much, but I still need to be careful, not to take so much my husband notices. I put everything in a large black garbage bag and hide it in the basement behind the furnace. D-Day finally arrives, I gather up my kids, take them to my bedroom, call Detroit Yellow Cab, and keep watch at the bedroom window. When I see the cab pull into the driveway, I pick up my daughter and tell my two sons to stay in the room until I call them. I walk down downstairs. My husband is sitting in the living room watching television. I walk past him, through the dining room, into the kitchen, down the basement staircase, and retrieve the garbage bag from behind the furnace. As I enter the living room, he looks up.

"What's that?" he asks.

"A garbage bag," I reply.

The cab driver sounds the horn. I open the front door and wave my hand to let him know I'm on my way out, and call my boys downstairs. For the first time in my marriage, I'm not afraid. I look my husband in the eyes; I do not turn away. I can't believe what I'm seeing: he actually looks sad. He begs me not to leave. I push the front door open wider, and he glances outside. The cab driver is watching. I see fear in my husband's eyes, not because of me but because a man is watching him. At that moment, I see my husband for what he is—a coward. He didn't have a problem hitting me when no one was around, but in the presence of another man, a stranger, sitting outside, inside a cab, he's afraid. All these years I've been afraid of a coward!

I secure my daughter on my right hip; pick up the garbage bag with my left hand; motion my sons out the door, down the front steps, and into the cab. As the cab backs out of the driveway onto the street, I look out the side window. My husband's standing on the front porch, his arms crossed atop his head, looking like he just got hit by a Mack truck. The cab driver stops at the stop sign at the end of the block looks both ways and proceeds. Suddenly, panic sets in; I hear a woman screaming. I look around the cab; no one appears to hear her screaming but me. Is that me? Am I the one screaming? The foul taste of vomit travels up my throat, spilling into my mouth.

"What the hell are you doing? STOP! You're making a BIG mistake! You're so stupid! You can't take care of yourself, let alone three kids! Tell the driver to turn around! Go back before it's too late!"

Great! Now, I'm talking to myself? I'm scared, but I know I can't go back! If I turn around, it will be ten times worse than before. I swallow the vile-vomit swooshing around inside my mouth; bite down on my lower lip as hard as I can, and the screaming stops. I look down at my baby girl resting peacefully on my lap, reach across the backseat, and pull my boys in closer. I don't know how I'm going to take care of them, but I do know we're never going back. My only recourse is my mom, returning to the house I couldn't wait to get out of. The thought of asking Mom for help is terrifying. What will she say? How will she react? But I need not have worried; Mom is still my mom; she greets us with open arms. No sly comments. No criticisms. No "I told you so's." No "maybe next time you'll listen." No a "hard head makes for a soft ass." The home I return to is not the house I ran away from.

Mom is so understanding, but then I'm no longer the defiant, disobedient sixteen-year-old teenager who couldn't wait to get away from her. I'm her daughter and a mother in need of help, just as she'd once been. She knows the struggles that lay ahead of me and promises to help as much as she can. But I'm not out of the woods yet. The familiar monsters of my childhood have returned. Years of abuse at the hands of a man I trusted with the painful secrets of my past have crippled me. The familiar whisperings of my failed life taunt me day and night.

"You're gonna fail and you're gonna take your kids down with you! You're worthless! You'll never amount to anything! Nobody wants you. Nobody loves you. Nobody ever will!"

Years later, my grown sons will recite the night I left their dad back to me in vivid detail. They were seven and five at the time. I fall asleep sick to my stomach. I don't know how to take care of myself; let alone three kids? But Mom keeps her promise. We have a roof over our head, shoes on our feet, clothes on our backs, and food in our bellies. She doesn't bring up my husband or ask why he isn't helping out financially. I'm fairly certain her past experience with deadbeat baby daddies has a lot to do with her silence. Mom doesn't complain, but after a few months, I can see the tow my children and I are having on her. Like my mom, I swallow my pride; call my husband, and ask for help. Like my dad, my husband says no but offers to take me back, no hard feelings and promises things will be different. I visualize myself going back and see my head bouncing off the living room wall. I hang up the phone and apply for ADC (Aid for Dependent Children).

Nowhere to turn, I return to the church. After a couple of weeks of attendance, I share my financial difficulties with the church mothers who suggest I volunteer for different church events and fundraisers whenever possible; they in turn promise to keep me appraised of job openings within the church. I make a point of making myself available for every church function and fundraiser. I serve food, clean pews, vacuum floors, wash walls, wash windows, wash dishes—whatever's in need of being done, I do. Several months pass, there's no mention of a job. I consider not returning but immediately dismiss the thought. I have one friend I talk with every now and then. I watch television and take care of my kids; attending church is the only time I get out of the house. Then one Sunday; sitting in church, squished between two pleasingly-plump sisters; bored out of my mind, something unbelievable happens. I hear a soft familiar voice, *Upon this rock I have built My church.*

It's a voice like no other; it's the voice of Jesus. I know it's the voice of Jesus because I heard it many years ago when I was just a girl. But I'm confused, He said, "I have built My church," not "I will build My church." What's He talking about? Aren't I sitting in His church? What rock? You can't build a church on a rock. Jesus takes form, smiles at me, and extends His right hand. At first, I think He's reaching out to me until I see a woman walking through the air toward Him. As she gets closer, I see her face. She kinda looks like me but doesn't. She's beautiful; she can't possibly be me. Surrounding her, stretching farther than my eyes can see, are rows and rows of the most beautiful people I have ever seen, all singing praises to the Lord; it is magnificent. Other than the lady who sorta, kinda looks like me and the countless people singing, the splendor of what I'm seeing reminds me of the first time I saw Jesus. I was eight years old hiding beneath my bed, praying the stepfather wouldn't see me.

Don't let him see me. Don't let him see me. Please, God, don't let him see me.

The stepfather leans down, lifts up the bottom of the bedspread, and looks under the bed. I close my eyes and wait for him to pull me out; nothing happens! I open my eyes; he's looking right at me but doesn't see me! How's that possible? I wave my hand in front of my face. Nothing! A voice calls to me from the closet; I don't know who it is, but I'm not afraid. I crawl from beneath my bed, make my way to the closet, and peek under the curtains; Momma hung curtains over the closet opening because there wasn't a closet door. I push aside the curtain and look inside; there's a wooden plank hanging midair as if it's being held, but there's no one there. I'm still not afraid; I crawl inside.

Directly behind the hanging plank is a small opening. Shining through the opening is the most beautiful light I've ever seen. I crawl through the opening; the space seems small at first, but the further I crawl, the larger it gets. I think this must be a magical place. At the center of the space is an enormous, pulsating gold-and-white light. Standing in the center is a man wearing a long white robe. And even though I've never seen him; I know, it's Jesus. And there's the most amazing aroma; an aroma I haven't smelled since; until today. I remember thinking then, as I do now, how did Jesus get so much stuff into such a small space? I recall looking out at my bedroom. The stepfather is still on his knees, looking under my bed, but I'm not there! *I'm not there!* I smile, curl up in Jesus' arms, and think to myself, *This must be what heaven feels and smells like.*

I look down at the congregation. I see myself seated in the pews, yet I'm suspended in midair. This is crazy! As I watch the bobbing heads, listen to the clapping hands, stomping feet, and mouths shouting "Jesus, hallelujah, amen," and the pastor frantically pacing back and forth across the podium—gasping, wheezing, and wiping the sweat from his brow with the large white silk handkerchief he's known for carrying (never could figure out why anyone would wipe sweat with silk; seemed to me a cotton handkerchief would have been better)—anyway, I couldn't help but wonder what would happen if all those head-bobbing, hand-clapping, foot-stomping, "Jesus, hallelujah, amen"—shouting Christians could see what I'm seeing and feel what I'm feeling.

Jesus opens His right hand. The lady who looks like me steps through the air into the palm of His hand. She doesn't look where she's going; her eyes are stayed; on Jesus. She's confident; she knows He won't let her fall. And man, can she sing! I can't sing, not even a little bit, never could. That's when it occurs to me; this can't be real! I'm hallucinating! I close my eyes, but it doesn't help, I can still smell that amazing aroma, and I can still hear her/me singing.

But that's not all. I can feel her. I can feel her love, joy, and confidence. I can feel the woman God designed me to be. The woman I now realize I can still be, if I so choose. At that moment, I know physically what I've always known spiritually. Jesus is the Rock, and I am His church. All my life, I thought the manmade building the world called church was the church Jesus was talking about. At that moment, in the blink of an eye, I became spiritually aware. At that moment, in the blink of an eye, everything returned to normal. I'm back in the *real* world; everything's *normal*. I'm bobbing my head, clapping my hands, stomping my feet, and shouting, "Jesus, halleluiah, amen!" Just like everybody else.

I want to tell everyone where I've been, what I saw and heard, but I'm afraid no one will believe me. People have always considered me somewhat odd. I seriously doubted my being older and having three kids had changed their opinion. I decide to keep what I "think" I saw, heard, and know to myself. Within a few days, it all seems like an impossible dream. After a few weeks, I decided I best let it go. Why wouldn't I? It's just like before; it wasn't real when I was eight years old; it isn't real now. Life is easier when you don't believe, and lies are far less painful than truth.

I eventually get a job cleaning motel rooms. It doesn't pay much, but added to what I'm receiving from ADC and Mom's generosity, I'm able to pay the security deposit and the first month on a lower-level two-family flat in Detroit; it's not in the best neighborhood, but thankfully it's not in the worse section of the city. One day, on the bus ride home, I overhear two women saying Chuck Muer's Seafood restaurant inside the Pontratrain Hotel is hiring and they hope to get hired. The following day, I take the Fort Street bus to downtown Detroit, walk to the Pontratrain Hotel, fill out a job application, get interviewed, and offered a waitressing position all on the same day! To my surprise, not only do I like waitressing, I'm actually, good at it. I make good tips and customers, and coworkers really seem to like me. No one has ever liked me; this was gonna take some getting used to.

Being on my own with three children, paying rent, utilities, buying food, clothes, and bus tickets to and from work, and my now ex-husband still refusing to pay child support, I'm bearly making ends meet. How the heck did Mom do this with seven kids? Man, I could really use Mom's help right about now, but she's already done so much; I need to figure this out on my own. I'm at my wit's end when I suddenly receive help from a disgruntled unexpected source, my customers. Restaurant policy states if a customer refuses their order, that order must be returned to the kitchen and replaced with a new order. If the server wants the order for him/herself, they can keep it. Those refused orders and whatever food my kids happen to leave on their plates become my daily meals. On the days I don't work, and if the kids don't leave any food on their plates, I don't eat. There simply wasn't enough food to feed both me and my kids. The one good thing that came from my lack of food, no weight problems, a claim I won't be able to make in my later years.

Tired of barely scraping by I take a page from momma's survival handbook and go back to school. I apply for financial aid, qualify for the Pell Grant, enroll at Wayne County Community College, graduate with an associate degree in child care technology, and immediately start looking for work. After several interviews, I realize I chose the wrong career. Why I "thought" my having been abused as a child somehow qualified me to work with abused children, I do not know. As a child care technician, I was expected to assist the caseworker assigned to the case with the reconciliation of the family. What! That wasn't in any of the textbooks or study sheets outlined in the child care technician syllabus! My brain implodes! I don't give a flying rat's behind about rehabilitating abusive parents so they can get their kids back! Lock 'em up! Lock 'em all up! And throw away the key! I don't care! No way am I lifting a finger to help them get back kids they lost! Needless to say, my job prospects go to zero.

I'm right back where I started, no way am I going back to making beds in smelly motel rooms and waiting tables, no way! I take a moment to consider my attributes. The only things I like to do are read, write, and draw. I determine writing is my best option. I transfer my college credits from Wayne County Community College to Madonna University. Three years later, I graduate with a bachelor of arts degree in journalism/public relations. Having completed the required internship at Channel 7 WXYZ to obtain my bachelor of arts degree I "assume" WXYZ will offer me a permanent position; I was wrong. I go on dozens of interviews with various television stations, radio stations, and local newspapers. But unlike the child care technology field, I'm not considered for a position. The reason is always the same—no job-related experience. How am I supposed to get job-related experience if no one's willing to hire me? Believing one of the media outlets will eventually hire me, I keep beating the media bushes! Nada! I decide to look for employment in nonrelated fields where my degree might work in my favor.

My determination and hard work finally pay off when I land a job as an admissions representative for a computer school. It's a far cry from the glamorous media career I envisioned, but a guaranteed salary, plus commission and bonuses more than make up for any disappointment I might be harboring. Talk about having your cake and eating it too; I'm a natural! I talk, people listen, and to my surprise, actually, take my advice. Within a few years, not only am I one of the top admissions representatives in the company, I'm also one of the highest-paid. No more counting pennies, no more cutting corners, no more robbing Peter to pay Paul; no more doing without. I can do whatever I want, buy whatever I want whenever I want, go wherever I want, eat whatever I want. Life is great! I give myself a great big pat on the back. Look at me! I can't believe I did all of this! I can't believe how successful I am! I can't believe how happy I am! Please note, "I can't believe "I" did all this!"

It never dawns on me; how could I possibly know I'm happy; considering I've never been happy. Is that even possible!—to have never been happy? I can remember every hurt, pain, and shame. Why can't I remember a single happy thing? Whatever! None of that matters anymore! The only thing that matters is here and now! And right now, I'm feeling pretty damn good! I can finally afford all the things the world said I'd never have. Things I thought were too good for people like me. Well, well, well, lookie-here; lookie-here, the times they are a-changing! I'm college-educated, I have a high-paying job, a brand-new car and I live in the suburbs! Don't get, no better, than that! Right? Wrong! Despite all I've been through, despite all I've seen and heard; I haven't learned a damn thing! All I think about is making money and buying more stuff! The more money, I make the more prosperous I look. The more prosperous, I look the more stuff I buy. The more stuff I buy, the more people like me. The more stuff I have, the more I like myself. Knowledge and wisdom have no place in my life.

I'm a naive child rummaging around in an immature adult body, making "gimme, gimme, gimme, spend, spend, spend" decisions. I never once think, maybe I should invest some of "my" money. Maybe I should set aside a portion of "my" earnings. Maybe one day "my" money will run out. Why, didn't any of those things ever occur to me? Why would they? I never had money before; other than spending it, I didn't have the faintest idea what to do with it. I never considered the downside. What kind of downside could there possibly be to having money?

Some might ask, "What about rainy days?"

My answer, what about um? My entire life has been rainy days! I'm done being rained on! I been struck by lightning so many times I lost count. No more! Let it rain! Let it rain! I'm making so much money I can stop the rain! If I can't stop it, so what! I make more than enough money to buy all the umbrellas I'll ever need! Life ain't got nothin on me! It's my turn to reign! Nothin's gonna stop me from gettin what's mine! Talk about—straight-up! Stuck on stupid! It's gonna take a minute/years, but I will *"consequently"* realize; worldly riches come at a mind-altering, soul demeaning, spirit-depleting cost.

When I was young and Mom got mad, she'd say stuff like, "I can show ya better than I can tell ya! Don't let yo mouth overload yo ass! Girl! I will slap the taste out yo mouth! Girl! I will beat the black off you. A hard head makes for a soft ass! You dun lost yo mind but umma help you find it! I brought you into this world, I can take you out!"

Momisms! Scary childrearing phrases passed down through the generations by black mothers to their hard-headed children to keep them in line. Mom never actually slapped the taste outa my mouth, beat the black off me, or "actually" threatened to kill me. She didn't have to; all she needed to do was make me believe she could and would. If Mom screamed one *-ism*, I prepared for a butt whoopin'. If she started stringing *-isms* together, one behind the other, I ran for my life. Mom's momism didn't just follow me throughout my child-hood; they followed me well into my adult life. The life I chose to live slapped the taste outa my mouth, beat the black off me, showed me better than it could tell me, killed me, only to revive me and do it all over again! Every time I lost my mind, life was right there to help me find it. As for my mouth; life made a point of overloading my ass—on a regular basis. I, actually thought, I was living, a pretty good life, until life showed me—just how ugly and cruel, it could be. Life kicked the crap out of me at my lowest and broke me just short of shattering during my in-betweens. Every time I "thought" I made it! Every time I "thought" my life was mine to live, as I pleased— life looped back-around and proved me wrong. I was so jacked-up I didn't know, truth from, lie. I didn't know who I was, why I was, or even if I was. Life was determined to destroy me, and it knew, the best way to do that was to take "my" stuff away! Stuff I "thought" was mine! Stuff "I" worked my a** off to get! Stuff "I" brought with "my" hard-earned money! Duh!

I am creature-comfort deaf and money blind. I can't hear evil's convincing whisperings for what they are; spiritual disarmament; self-annihilation of the soul. I can't see he's been manipulating and cataloging my life choices since I was a child. Measuring my anger and want; weighing how far I will go to get what I "think" I deserve. Calculating how much of my soul I will sacrifice to hold on to "my" stuff. Creature comforts have made me proud and arrogant, but that's all about to change.

"Pride goeth before destruction, and a haughty spirit before the fall." 1st Peter 5:5

Woe unto me! I'm about to have the rug pulled out from under me by God's biblical truths. A fool and his/her money are soon parted; the love of money is the root of *all* evil. The Lord giveth, the Lord taketh away. How the mighty have fallen. God's people are destroyed for lack of knowledge. There are a lot more bible scriptures about fools and money, but I'm fairly certain, you get the picture.

Had I taken just a modicum of time to acquire a modicum of knowledge, I would have been better prepared for the years to come. I'm destroying myself, but I'm unwilling to change. When I was a child, Mom called this kind of behavior cutting off your nose to spite your face. Stupid! Stupid! Stupid! Bitterness, self-pity, and suspicion reinforced my blindness. I'm so busy looking for the wrong in others; I can't see the wrong in me. I can't see the person I'm becoming. Yet despite my mistrust of Christians and preachers, I keep going to church. Why? Because, regardless of how I feel about Christians and preachers, I know beyond a shadow of a doubt God is responsible for my financial good fortune. How do I know? I know because I graduated from Wayne Community College with an associates degree, transferred those credits to Madonna University, obtained a bachelor's degree, and make close to $100,000 a year, never having graduated high school.

How's that possible? Short answer—Divine Providence. When I enrolled at Wayne Community College, no one asked to see my high school diploma or requested my high school transcripts. When I transferred my credits to Madonna University, admissions assumed I graduated high school because I had an associate's degree. When I attended Detroit public schools, my grades were never higher than a C or D, yet I graduated from Wayne Community College and Maddona University with high GPAs. Some might call this luck or human error; I call it God's divine intervention. Yet even though I know this is true, I'm unwilling to give God credit for "my" success. What I am willing to give Him is money. I might be stupid, but I'm not so stupid I don't pay my tithes. I know the consequences of not tithing. Every sermon I've ever heard ends the same way—hell's fire and brimstone! Give unto God what is God's or pay the price!

"Bring your tithes to the storehouse! Give unto Cesar what is Caesar's! Give unto God what is God's! As you sow, so shall you reap. God loves a cheerful giver. If you don't sow, you won't reap. When you don't pay your tithes, you're stealing from God! God knows your heart! God knows! God knows!" Blah, blah, blah! These "encouraging words" were usually followed by one or more terrifying Bible stories of what befell those who didn't pay their tithes—primarily death. Every pastor preached the same thing: not paying your tithes is stealing from God.

"Are you a thief, brothers and sisters? Thieves will be dealt with according to the Word of God!"

The more I attend "church," the more cynical I'm becoming. The preacher's threatening scriptures go in one ear and out the other. My two sons are grown and gone; my daughter is the only one still living at home. I'm making more money than I ever dreamed possible; tithing isn't a problem. I always give more than the required 10 percent as well as a generous offering.

I promised at the very beginning to only speak the truth. Therefore, truthfully speaking, my present truth bears no resemblance to my past truth. That being said, I wouldn't change a single thing. To change who I was in the past would change who I am in the present. I would no longer be who I am, and I rather like the woman I've become. Oftentimes, it's dark truths that light the darkness and prove the most relatable and beneficial. I've done and said a lot of things I'm ashamed of, but dwelling on things that can't be undone or unsaid won't change a thing. However, learning from those things, using those things to teach, help, comfort, and enlighten others changes everything.

My dark truth. During my dark years, everything I did, said, and thought was an affront to God, but never once, did I question His existence. What I questioned was God's why. Why He let so many terrible things happen? Why He didn't do something? Why He didn't say something? When people called Him a lie, a figment of the imagination, a made-up fairytale or accused Him of not caring, why didn't He prove Himself? He saw how broken we were; why didn't He fix us? Why didn't He stop us from hurting and killing one another? Why didn't He get rid of the bad people and just keep the good? Why didn't He get rid of decease, pain, and suffering? Why did He let the innocent die and the guilty keep living? Why did He give us free will knowing we'd misuse it? Why did He make bad people rich and good people poor? Why didn't He make us all the same so we could love one another?

When I thought about my childhood, all those years of hurt, pain, and shame—knowing there was an all-powerful, all-knowing, all-hearing, all-seeing, God who could have saved me, but chose not to; messed me up in ways I can't begin to describe. Yes, it was men who molested me. Yes, it was those I loved and trusted who betrayed me. But it was God who created them! He was responsible for them! He could have stopped them! He should have stopped them! I determined the ones who hurt me and those who stood around watching must have been sick in the head but not God! Nothing was wrong with Him! No way was I letting Him off the hook! He wasn't messed up in the head, but He stood around watching like everyone else, never saying a word, never lifting a finger! He's the Creator! He created everything! Why did He create people He knew would do such horrible, unthinkable things? I will never forgive Him for what He let happen to me. That should have been the end of it, right? Wrong! God sends His Son!

For seven days my life was perfect; my life was complete. Jesus says He loves me. He tells me I'm loved, I'm beautiful, I'm special; that I should not fear. When I'm with Him, there is no pain, no sorrow, no fear, no shame! He hides me in the midst of the stepfather. I walk past him throughout the day, but he doesn't see me. I'm *invisible*! Everybody else in the house sees me; they even talk to me but not the stepfather. I think to myself, *How is this even possible?* Jesus and I laugh and talk nonstop. We sing, run, jump and spin in circles, lay in plush emerald-green meadows, and watch white wispy clouds float by. We wade in the sparkling blue lakes and clear shimmering streams and run through rainbow waterfalls. For seven amazing days and nights, I walk hand in hand with Jesus. Consumed by His love, and kindness. I see as He sees. I see the earth God created; before the pollutants of men. For the first time in my life, I know I'm loved. Until, one day, the unimaginable happens; Jesus tells me, He's leaving.

*****

It was as if the stepfather somehow knew Jesus was gone. I sat paralyzed on the edge of my bed. He walked into the room, stopped in front of me, looked right at me, and I knew—I wasn't invisible anymore. My life returned to what it was. I returned to what I was—nothing. My heart sank, why did Jesus do this? Why did He leave me here? Why didn't He take me with Him? What did I do? I wish I didn't know Him. I wish He never came. I wish I didn't know there was a better place—a place beyond the tears, hurt, pain, and shame. For seven days, Jesus hid me, comforted me, said He loved me. What kind of love is that? What kind of love does this? If this is how love feels, Jesus can take it back! I don't won't no part of it! I don't won't no part of Him! I will never forget His parting words, *You will not know happiness until your later years.*

*****

I'm eight years old! Who tells an eight-year-old kid something like that? Later years! What the heck are later years? And *poof,* He's gone! Leaving me just as He found me, with one painful exception. I now have intimate knowledge of Him, knowledge of His power, knowledge I didn't have before. Jesus is gone, but His mysterious words remain: "You will not know happiness until your later years." I'm so messed up! I know Jesus is real! I believed Him! I trusted Him! He said He loved me! He's a liar! He can't be trusted! He doesn't love me! He NEVER loved me! How could He? He knows what I am. He knows I'm bad!—bad like all the bad things done to me. If I weren't bad, bad things wouldn't keep happening to me. It slowly dawns on me—Jesus thinks the bad things were my fault! I'm never trusting anyone again. If I don't trust anyone; I won't get hurt. I was wrong.

Shortly after my twelfth birthday, I decide once school lets out for the summer, I'm running away. By the time summer rolls around, enough time has passed for me to realize running away isn't the answer. Where can I go? The police will just find me and bring me back, and there's "stranger danger." Be careful when you're outside playing; watch out for strangers, if a stranger tries to talk to you or grab you—Run! Scream for help as loud as you can. Don't stop running; don't stop screaming until somebody comes to your rescue! Yeah! Right! What a joke! My stranger danger lived inside, not outside, and he wasn't a stranger; he was a familiar. I'd been running, screaming for help, and waiting for someone to rescue me since I was eight. Nobody saw me running. Nobody heard me screaming. Nobody came to my rescue. That's when it hit me; I could live with my real father. He isn't a good man, but he's my real dad, at least I'd be safe with him.

The pain my dad caused when he abandoned us still hurts. Maybe he's changed; maybe he'll be happy to see me; maybe he'll want me now, maybe. I don't know how I'm supposed to feel about my dad; I only know living with him has to be better than living with the stepfather. It takes about a week for me to muster up enough courage to ask Mom if I live with my dad. Once I do, she laughs, cocks her head to the side, asks me if I lost my mind, and says no! No explanation, no discussion, no nothin', just no, but I didn't care; I wasn't about to give up. I spend the next two weeks doing anything and everything to make Momma's life miserable, and it works; she finally agrees to let me visit my dad. Visit? I think to myself, *Whatever, Ma! I just want out of here!* I'll talk Daddy into letting me stay once I get there. The stepfather is so pissed; I don't think I've ever seen him so angry, but there's nothing he can do or say. I'm finally getting out, and I'm never coming back.

Freedom is only one day away but seems to be taking forever. Nothing in my life suggest prayer, actually works, but I pray anyway, pray for just one night of uninterrupted sleep. Word of Momma's sewing skills had spread throughout the neighborhood and church congregation. Knowing how much Momma loves sewing, the stepfather suggests she uses her sewing to make herself a little chump change. Before long, Momma was getting sewing orders from all over town, most of Momma's appointments had to be set in the evening after the stepfather got off work so he could drop her off and pick her back up. But not today! Today is the day before tomorrow. Tomorrow is my freedom day! Tomorrow is my birthday, Christmas, Thanksgiving, and the Fourth of July all rolled into one. Tomorrow, I break out of this jailhouse, pretending to be a home. Tomorrow, my prison sentence finally comes to an end. Momma didn't schedule any appointments for today or tomorrow; she's going to spend the next couple of days doing my hair and helping me pack my nicest clothes. Mom wants me to look my absolute best for my deadbeat dad; she and the stepfather are taking me to the Greyhound bus station tomorrow. Tomorrow is the last day I have to look at his face, smell his Pall Mall-cigarette breath, or gag on his Old Spice cologne. I'm so happy! It feels like I'm gonna explode! Tonight I fall asleep unafraid! No squeaking floorboards and creaking door hinges, no hushes in the night. Tomorrow, I wake up free!

I can't remember the last time I woke up this happy; if ever. Little did I know, I was about to learn the parable of chickens, "Don't count yo eggs before they hatch." Momma packs me a week's worth of clothes and a brown bag lunch; two baloney-and-cheeses sandwiches, four windmill cookies, and we're out the door to the Greyhound bus station; the stepfather keeps looking at me in the rearview mirror. I turn my head and look out the side window. I don't turn my head back around until we reach the bus station. Mom and the stepfather walk to the counter and purchase a one-way bus ticket; Daddy agreed to purchase my ticket back. Daddy lives somewhere in Ohio, so I won't be on the bus for too long.

It's finally time to board the bus! I'm excited and terrified. How can I be excited and terrified at the same time? Afraid of what I'll see if I look in the stepfather's direction, I keep my head down and my eyes focused on the ground. As I'm boarding the bus, I feel momma's hands on my shoulders. She turns me around, looks me in the eyes, tells me to behave myself, leans down, gives me a hug, a quick kiss on the forehead; then quickly wipes the dark red lipstick away with her thumb. I love momma so much, I'm gonna miss her, but I can't stay here. If I stay here um gonna die. Besides, she has five other daughters; she'll be okay without me. I wasn't worried about my sisters or my brother; the stepfather didn't seem to be interested in anyone but me. The bus fills up quickly, not a single empty seat, not a single familiar face. For the first time in as long as I can remember; I feel safe. I'm not hungry but decide to eat my windmill cookies anyway. They taste different! Way, better than at home! I never imagined freedom could taste—Soooooooooooo Good!

The first few days with Daddy are wonderful! He introduces me to his stable/four women; they're so nice. They comb my hair, paint my fingernails and toenails, buy me candy, play duck duck goose with me, and they talk to me like I matter. They even say I'm pretty; the stepfather is the only one at home who calls me pretty; everyone else says I look like my dad. But nobody liked my dad, so where did that leave me? Afraid of what I might see, I never look at myself in the mirror. I do everything with my eyes closed, wash my face, comb my hair, brush my teeth, as far as I was concerned, there was nothing to see, nothing pretty anyway.

I'm fairly certain daddy's women are being kind; more so for him; than me, but I don't care; real or fake, it's better than I'm use to getting. Then late one night, it all falls apart. The ladies are out working. There's a knock at the door; Daddy answers. I hear him talking to a man followed by footsteps walking down the hall. The bedroom door opens; the ceiling light flicks on; a tall man walks to the foot of the bed; looks down at me; turns around; looks at my dad; and says, "I don't f—k little girls."

I look at the man's clenched fist; was he going to hit my dad? He stares at daddy for a few more seconds, pushes past him, stomps his way down the hall, and out the backdoor; slamming it shut behind him. I will later wonder how he could be so upset, and not report daddy to the police. Over time, I come to realize, it wasn't in him to rescue me. That though he was angered by daddy's offer of "me"; once his anger passed, he would return to the rundown, paint-peeling house, at the end of the dead-end street, to buy what daddy was selling.

The following day, I tell Daddy I want to go home. He doesn't apologize for the night before, doesn't ask why I'm leaving early, doesn't ask me to stay; just tells me to get my stuff, drives me to the bus station, buys my ticket back to Detroit, tells me to wait in the lobby until the bus boards and leaves. No I love you, no hugs, no kisses, no goodbye, no looking back. Suddenly, I'm six years old, standing on the train station platform in Birmingham, Alabama, holding my Momma's hand, watching my daddy drive away. The bus ride back to Detroit seems quicker than the bus ride leaving Detroit. I step from the bus onto the pavement; Momma and the stepfather are waiting. The stepfather takes my suitcase, hugs me, and says, "We missed you. Nothing was the same without you."

But what he's really saying is he missed me; things are exactly the same; nothing has changed. I decide not to tell Mom what hap-

pened in Ohio. If nothing else my short escape from reality—reaf-
firmed my reality. There's no such thing as freedom. Once a prisoner
always a prisoner. What the stepfather and everyone else says about
me is true: I'm just like my dad. Why else would he try to sell me?
I didn't know how mom would react if I told her what happened
in Ohio. I only knew I was afraid what the stepfather said was true;
that momma loved him more than me. So I did what the stepfather
trained me to do; I kept my mouth shut.

Toward the end of summer, the Baker family moves into the
house across the street. They look like one of those Norman Rockwell
paintings—all happy, clean and shiny. The mother is beautiful; the
father is handsome; and their three little girls are adorable. About a
week after they move in, word gets around that Mrs. Baker is looking for a babysitter. She works nights; Mr. Baker works days; none
of their daughters are school-age; they need someone responsible
to watch them in the evening and possibly sleepover a few nights a
week. Every age-appropriate girl in the neighborhood interviews for
the job, but Mrs. Baker likes me best. I think to myself, things are
finally looking up. But I thought wrong; things are about to go from
bad to really bad.

The Bakers are everything my biological family and the stepfather isn't. They're married; they don't argue, cuss, smoke, or drink.
They don't have weekend gambling parties, and they don't attend
church. Their life is like Osie and Harriet Nelson, backyard Bar-b-
ques, trips to the ice cream parlor, sitting in the living room watching television and eating popcorn, biking and long family car rides.
Mrs. Baker kisses her husband goodbye every morning before he
leaves for work, and Mr. Baker always makes it home in time to eat
dinner with the family before Mrs. Baker leaves for her evening job;
they're the perfect family. Even on the days I'm not babysitting, I'm
at the Baker's. Within a few weeks, I'm spending most of my nights
at their house, returning home the following morning in time to get
dressed for school. Most school days, Mrs. Baker makes me breakfast
before I head home. I'm actually starting to like my life a little bit.

I'm rarely home during the evening anymore; the stepfather is fit-to-be-tied but doesn't say anything for fear of being found out.

I feel safe with Mr. Baker, he's a father I can trust, he's the father I deserve; the father I always imagined. I decide to tell him my dark secret. Mr. Baker's a strong man; it will take a strong man to stop the stepfather. I'm nervous and happy. Nervous about what I'm about to share; happy someone other than me will finally know my dark secret—happy the nightmare will soon be over. I ask Mr. Baker if I can talk to him; he smiles and says, of course. I take a deep breath, open my mouth, and the words spill out like a rushing flood. I don't think I took another breath until I finished telling Mr. Baker every painful thing the stepfather did to me. Once I'm done talking, I take my second deep breath and ask Mr. Baker if he will help me. He doesn't say a word, just sits there staring at me.

That's when I saw it, the face I've seen every night of my life since I was eight. Mr. Baker pats his knee with his right hand and motions me to him with his left. Time stops, no tears, no pain, no shame, no fear, no anger, no trying to reason why. As I walk toward him, my last glimmer of hope fades to black; there's nothing left of me. I close my eyes and brace for the incoming thrust; maybe this is all there is for nothing little girls like me. I try to imagine myself somewhere else, but my brain isn't working. I'm trapped inside reality; there's no imaging in here. Before tonight, I had a safe place, a place without question, pain, or shame, a meticulously spun imaginary life, protected inside an impenetrable cocoon of my design and making.

It's a good pretend life; I get to be someone else—someone who isn't afraid, someone who doesn't cry, someone who doesn't feel hurt or pain, someone who does not cower in the face of danger. I'm brave, I'm fearless, I'm a warrior. I slay dragons and demons; I protect the innocent. As my physical body lay helpless in the outside world, I fought fearlessly from within; in a land far, far away. Tonight I fear I will never find my way back; to my imaginary place. My brave, imaginary nightlife brought me imaginary joy throughout the pretense of day. Imaginings taught me how to protect, myself, from further damage, how to recognize the enemy. I know my enemy; I know where he lives. I know his tricks and those of his advocates. His true character is etched in my soul; I never thought to look elsewhere. I never imagined the enemy living in a "safe" place surrounded by love and kindness. I never imagined the enemy could change form. I never imagined rape could disguise itself as kindness. I never imagined I would need my imaginings with Mr. Baker. I was wrong. Everything happened so fast I didn't have time to spin my imaginary cocoon. I never made it to my safe imaginary place.

As I imagined, Mr. Baker, my knight in shining armor, he pretended to be the father I always wanted. I imagined myself into believing I was safe, imagined Mr. Baker would become so enraged by what I told him he'd call the police, the stepfather would go to jail; the Bakers would adopt me and I would live happily ever after. Tonight I realize and accept there's no such thing as happily ever after, just more of the same, inside a different house, atop a different bed, at the mercy of a man who doesn't look like the stepfather yet is. But all is not lost. God sometimes sends His rescuer in the form of a child.

One night, a few months after telling Mr. Baker my secret, I see his daughter Teresa peeking at us through a crack in his bedroom door. When she sees me looking at her, she lowers her head and backs away. Once Mr. Baker's done with me, he sends me to his daughter's bedroom, which is where I sleep when I stay over. The girls have the largest bedroom; their three pink and lavender beds and, white chest of drawers take up most of the space, but Mrs. Baker arranged their beds and dresser, in such a way, the girls had plenty of room to play. I tip-toe down the upstairs hallway to the girl's bedroom. Other than the moonlight streaming through the bedroom window, the room is completely dark. I navigate my way through the darkness without bumping into anything or stepping on any toys. As I slide into the sleeping bag Mrs. Baker brought me, I breathe a sigh of relief, but not for long. I'm being watched.

Afraid to look up, hoping and praying I'm wrong, I slowly turn my head toward the moonlight. It takes my eyes a few seconds to adjust to the dark; to my relief the girls are asleep; all but one—Teresa. My head is pounding, I feel sick to my stomach, shame consumes me. What's she still doing up? She can't possibly understand what she saw. Can she? No way! She's just a little girl. Yet, at that moment, as we sat staring at one another in the darkness; the moonlight caressing her innocent face, she seems older, wise beyond her years. We don't speak, we can't speak, there are no words. Teresa lays down in her bed and pulls the covers above her head. I scoot down in my sleeping bag as far as I can; wishing I could zip myself away. I fall asleep afraid; not knowing what tomorrow will bring. My dreams are overrun by nightmares; dreadful rememberings of yesteryear; recollections of scary, painful, unthinkable things. Scary, painful, unthinkable things I was too young to know, but somehow recognized. I was only eight-years-old; I didn't know how to put the scary, painful, unthinkable things into words. Teresa is much younger than I was—hopefully, she's too young to understand what she saw. But I was wrong. Unbeknownst to me, come tomorrow, this little girl will do what no adult was willing to do; what I was too afraid and ashamed to do for myself—she will come to rescue me.

Teresa, who normally lays in bed until being told, no less than four times to get up, gets up on her own, puts on her slippers, walks to the hallway, and proceeds downstairs. I quickly follow. She walks into the kitchen. Mr. and Mrs. Baker are seated at the breakfast table laughing and drinking their morning cup of coffee. Theresa hurries past her dad without saying a word, her eyes laser-focused on her mom. Mr. Baker calls out to her, but she doesn't turn around. Tears streaming down her small face, Teresa tells her mom what she saw her dad doing to me. I don't know what to do. Do I stay? Do I run? Do I scream? Do I cry? Before I can make up my mind what to do, Mrs. Baker turns and looks at me; our eyes lock. She looks so sad. What have I done?

I look over at Mr. Baker. He doesn't look handsome anymore; he looks sick. He's sweating and trembling. His caramel skin looks drained and sickly. Mrs. Baker doesn't say anything to her husband. She pushes her chair back from the table, tells me to get dressed, and go home. Later that day, I see Mr. Baker loading boxes and clothes into the trunk of his car. A few weeks later, a moving truck pulls up to the Baker house. I watch from the front-room window as movers carry boxes, clothes, and furniture from the house to the back of the truck. When I see the couch, dining table, and chairs being loaded onto the truck, I know the movers are nearly done. I run down the backstairs, out the door, around the side of the house, and across the street. The Baker girls see me coming and let out a high-pitched squeal. As I step from the street onto the curb, they wrap their tiny arms around my legs; refusing to let me go. I know I'll never see them again, but it's okay; they're safe now. Mrs. Baker smiles, wraps her arms around me, kisses my forehead, and whispers in my ear, "I'm so sorry, Toni. Thank you for taking such good care of my girls."

Shortly after Mrs. Baker and her girls move away the stepfather moves out. I'm happy but confused. I know God is somehow involved in this; what I don't know is why. A million questions flood my still young immature mind, but none of them will be answered until my later years.

My Latter Years

It was amid my stolen youth; my fragmented soul-wrenching moments, buried deep inside my sorrow and shame; the alone, confused, angry; afraid moments; moments I thought no one saw, no one heard; no one cared. It was here amid my brokenness that God sowed His Sustenance. My Restoration; my Recommence—Wholly Complete; Abundantly Sufficient. Spirit to spirit to soul. Comforting Reinsurance; God's plans to prosper me and not to harm me; to give me hope and a future. Plans so Wholly-Complete; so Abundantley Sufficient they overshadowed my limited understanding. As God saw fit; I would not discern His plans until; my latter years. In my latter years I realize, nothing I did or said; nothing others did or said regarding me. Nothing I subsequently do or say; nothing others subsequently do or say regarding me changes how God sees or feels about me. Knowing these things reassures me time and time again; God's, Sacrifice, Grace and Mercy are greater than my sin.

In my latter years, I hear the anguish in Christs' voice when He said, *"You will not know happiness until your latter years."*, anguish lost amid the misunderstanding of a terrified little girl. Only during my latter years do I understand, though my physical innocence was taken, my spiritual innocence remained untouched. That God's ways are not my ways. Though His will never changes, His ways change continually for my good benefit. Only then do I discern, no matter how much God wants me to be happy, no matter how much He wants to keep me safe, He cannot, under any circumstances, interfere with my free will/choices or that of those connected to me. Whether my choices be for or against me or for or against others, God cannot change or prevent my choices nor can He change or prevent the choices of others regarding me.

In my latter years, I understand the excellence of God's intervention—that He intervenes respectful of my free will/choices. If I choose badly, the consequences of my bad choice must play out. God will not interfere; He cannot stop what I put in motion. And therein dwells our problem, brothers and sisters. If we choose wrongly, God cannot use that wrong choice for our good benefit or the good benefit of others until after the wrong choice is made. Even then, the good resulting from God's intervention might not manifest for years, which is what happened to me when I was a child. Someone made an evil choice, and I paid the price. Years later, others benefited from the price I paid.

In my latter years, I don't just look, I see. I don't just hear, I listen. I stop making excuses and start taking responsibility. I stop blaming others and start celebrating myself! I am who I am in spite of the bad, not because of the bad. I pay homage to the brave little girl whose tremblings, pain, and suffering laid the steadfast foundation upon which I now stand. I see her childhood scars for what they were and continue to be—victories in the making. I've been blessed to see the cause of every bad thing in my life; as I have been blessed to see the resulting good beyond my life. I see Jesus standing beside me amid every trial, tribulation, heartache, and heartbreak. I bear witness to the bountiful harvest of my soiled childhood: three beautiful, strong, compassionate, independent women; devoted mothers who would have withered and died little girls on a vine, had I not survived the strangling weeds of my childhood.

I see God choose me, His wounded sacrifice, His secret weapon. I see Him hide me in plain sight. I see angels watching over me. When I was six years old, my biological father gave evil reason to take notice of me. When evil turned to see what my biological father discarded, it saw despair, weakness, and fear—a nothing, inconsequential, powerless little girl. Evil was wrong.

In my latter years, I discern what it means to have God's trust, trust I couldn't understand as a child. I was only a child, yet God trusted and believed in me. I did not know what I was capable of; God did. God knew when the time came I would sacrifice myself without hesitation. He chose me to protect three innocent lambs, three little girls who would not have survived the unnatural desires of their father. He chose me because I knew the enemy. He chose me because I had endured and survived the demons of child molestation for four years of my twelve-year life. He chose me, no longer innocent, no longer pure, to protect the innocent and pure. He chose me because He knew I would prevail. He chose me because He designed me to live, not die. But I'm just a child. I have no knowledge or understanding of these things. It is because I have no knowledge or understanding of these things that I hate God. It is because God knows I have no knowledge or understanding of these things that He loves me all the more.

God knows my hatred will grow and fester beyond childhood, but He also knows there's an appointed time and season still to come. He knows, within this appointed time and season, my heart will soften, my pain will quiet, my shame will fade, my anger will lessen, my bitterness will melt. Within this appointed time and season, not a moment sooner, not a moment later, a patch of frozen, contaminated soul, will thaw, become fertile and ripe for planting. My eyes are open to see; my ears are open to listen; and suddenly I know, God wastes nothing, even the most horrific things work together for good. Everyone and everything under God's Son has a divine purpose.

In my latter years, I realize life was never about me finding a "way" around, over, though, or out. It was about me opening my heart and letting; the Way in. Letting the Way lead me. Letting the Way reveal; God's Purpose for my life. In the presence of His Purpose, I grow in knowledge, wisdom, and understanding. Amid His Purpose, revelation blankets me, truth beckons me, I drink from the spring of living waters; dance amid fields of Grace and Mercy. I am anxious for nothing. My dead barren places are alive and thriving; showing no evidence of ever having been dead or barren. But alas, God knows these things will not manifest until my latter years, and so, He does what a forgiving, merciful Father does, He waits patiently—for my hatred of Him to ease.

In my latter years, my soul comprehends what it was incapable of understanding as a child: The power of sacrifice. The Sacrificial Power I unknowingly tapped into when I was eight-years-old. The Power that mounted up on wings of eagles in my defense. The Power that survived my painful, demoralizing childhood. The Power that wiped away my tears, night after night. The Power that constantly whispered in my ear, *"What God gives no man can take away."* The Power of the Holy Spirit.

I lost sight of God so many times during my life, but not once did He lose sight of me. In my latter years, I recognize God's truth. It is amid His truth, that I recognize, me. Not the me others say I am. Not the me I pretend I am. I recognize the me God says I am. The me I was authored, designed, and created to be. I discern childhood battles preparing me for adult wars. I discern the sufferings of my childhood with a new understanding—my God allowed sufferings. Sufferings, for such a time as then—for such a time as this. I see clearly. I listen attentively. I know absolutely! There is no life without sacrifice! There is no sacrifice without life!

I am a new creature in Christ. I am Moses Esther. Things difficult to understand prior to this appointed time and season present themselves simply and completely, causing me to ponder, was it always this simple? Did I not want to see, not want to listen, not want to feel? I see the impact of my selfish actions, hear the resound of my brash words, feel the heaviness of my inconsiderate choices. How could I have been so blind, so deaf, so unfeeling? How could I, without forethought, disregard my obligations and responsibilities to humankind? How could I not recognize the longing within me, the inborn yearning for my brothers and sisters; every man, woman, and child; every race, ethnicity, creed, and nationality. How could I not...

I confess!—I'm incomplete because I chose to be incomplete. Only after confessing this truth do I discern and accept my obligation to the "whole" of humanity. Only after accepting my responsibility to the "whole" do I surrender "completely" unto Christ. Only by way of Him; the Way, the Truth, and the Life; am I made whole and complete. I further confess—I am the obstacle standing in my way. I am my problem. Christ is my solution. And suddenly I know—my obstacle/myself; everything in my life; be it manmade, self-made, or God allowed, *"must"* align with my God-Given-Purpose. Anything "not" aligned with my God-Given-Purpose; finding no safe dwelling within me; must flee.

Only after confessing these things do I understand the Accountability Factor of free will—that God didn't put conditions on our free will, He put conditions on us! His children!—We the people! Had God put conditions on free will, it would not be free; it wouldn't be, our will, be done, it would be, God's will be done—do as we're told. Without question. So what did God do? He did what any loving Father does to protect His children; He gave His children chores to fulfill and rules to follow. How are those chores and rules taught, learned, and enforced? The bible. Scripture, God's written word, biblical laws, commandments, statutes, ordinances, decrees, and precepts. Therein making us responsible for our free will, the choices we make.

When God gifted us free will, He gave His word, not to inter-fere in our choices. Still being a Loving Father, knowing the carnal nature of His children, our capacity for sin, He also gifted us grace and mercy. But that's not all He did; He sent the Holy Spirit to Earth to comfort, teach, guide, and give us reason to pause during times of choice. Still, good, bad, or indifferent, our choices are our own; we are responsible for the outcome of our choices, not God, not Jesus, not the Holy Spirit, not Lucifer, not family, not friends, not enemies not society. How we "choose" to utilize our free will falls entirely to us! We alone are responsible for our choices! No matter how many bad choices we make, no matter how much pain we inflict, no mat-ter how much devastation we cause, God gave His word—not to interfere. So what if God doesn't like the choices we're making! It's not like He can revoke our free will! Take back what He gave us. Nope! Not happening! Good, bad, right, wrong, or indifferent; God is stuck with our free will/choices. Our Saving Grace, "All things work together for good." Romans 8:25. Should truth who is God, and God who is truth go back on His Word, one word remains, *poof!* Everybody! Everything! Gone! Forever! Never! Ever! Coming back!

The very nature of life affirms we're going to make bad choices and mistakes. Yet, it's the choices we make after those bad choices and mistakes that affirm the character of who we are. Some of us will blame our bad choices and mistakes on others—he/she made us do it. Some of us won't care, some of us will make the best of the bad choice/mistake we made, some of us will try to make amends, some of us will ask for help, some of us will ask for forgiveness, some of us will run, some of us will hide, some of us will pretend it never happened, some of us will learn from our bad choices/mistakes and try to do better, some of us will pray. Once we run out of people, places, and things to blame we'll turn our attention to the supernatural; heaven, hell, God, the devil. Really?

The truth of the matter is, blaming others for our bad choices/ mistakes, makes no sense. The consequence of a bad choice/mistake "always" falls to the one who made it. Why?—free will/choice. God gave us "individual" free will; not group free will. I can't choose for you. You can't choose for me. I'm not responsible for your choices. You're not responsible for my choices. As for the bad choices and mistakes of others that advertently or inadvertently affect us; we decide as "individuals" how we choose to react. Of one thing I'm certain; bad choices/mistakes do not, under any circumstances, excuse, justify, or legitimize, like-responses. *"Do not repay evil with evil or insult with insult. On the contrary, repay evil with blessing, because to this you were called so that you may inherit a blessing.* 1 Peter 3:9

As for God somehow being responsible for our bad choices/ mistakes. Really? The One who gave us free will and gave His word not to interfere; the Beginning and the End, Alpha and Omega; what was, is, and forever will be. Pretty sure He has more important things to do with His time than jerk us around. The devil, double really? He can only do as much as we allow him to do. He isn't God; he doesn't have the power or authority to be everywhere at once. Only God has the power and authority to be everywhere, simultaneously. Only God is omnipresent. Don't get me wrong, I'm no fan of Satan, but he gets blamed for a lot of stuff we do to ourselves. Lord knows he left me on autopilot for more years than I care to admit. There was no need for him to do anything to me; I was doing far more damage to myself than he ever could.

God has given me so much over the years, but my most favorite thing is tender mercies. Despite the pain I caused myself and others, God loved me enough to let me learn from my bad choices and mistakes. I learned the true tragedy of bad choices and mistakes isn't the bad choice or the mistake. Once made; neither can be changed. The true tragedy of bad choices and mistakes is the countless tragedies that will follow if I do not learn from my bad choices and mistakes. The people I will never help if I do not learn. The life lessons I never teach and share if I do not learn. The positive role model I will never become if I do not learn. The positive examples I will never set if I do not learn. The greatest tragedy of all, the tragic reality that I will continue making the same bad choices and mistakes again and again because I did not care enough to learn. Because I did not care enough about others; my brothers and sisters; to learn. Because I did not care enough to take responsibility for my words and actions.

In my latter years, yielding to social pressure, bartering for acceptance, false promises, fake gestures, lies, and the opinions of others run their course, and I finally realize the world is insatiable. The more I give of myself, the more it wants; it will never be satisfied. Once I realize this, I also realize though I am in the world, I can no longer be a part of it. Only after realizing these things about myself do I take ownership of myself, stop lying to myself about myself, stop thinking the world owes me something, stop looking at what others are doing to me and start seeing what I'm doing to myself, stop hearing what others are saying about me and start listening to what I am secretly saying about myself. I look and I see the pivotal role I played in my misery. I begin to see myself in others and others in myself. I discern the peace and conflict of free will and understand the centuries-old battle between the forces good and evil raging within me. I stop straddling the fence and choose Christ as he chose me—unconditionally.

In my latter years, I am made aware I have God-given authority and power—the power to command battlefields, the authority to cast out demons, the power to cast down whatever rises up against me! The authority rise up the tides of war! The authority to cast down the tides of war! Nothing on Earth, in heaven, or hell can choose for me. I must choose for myself. I choose love over hate. I choose good over evil. I choose right over wrong. I choose forgiveness over unforgiveness. I choose empathy over apathy. I choose a life service over a life of disservice. I choose us! The world didn't make me! The world can't break me! More importantly; the world didn't make us. The world can't break us—unless we allow!

When I was a child, evil people chose for me. When I became a teenager, I chose defiantly. When I became a teenage mother, I chose foolishly. When I became a teenage wife, I lacked the learned knowledge to choose correctly. When I became a single parent, I choose recklessly. Having nowhere to turn to, I return to the church. Not because I believe or disbelieve, not because I thought the church could or would help but because that's what I was raised to do: when you don't know what to do, when you have nowhere to go, go to church.

My life was a mess! I didn't know who I was or what I was. I often wished I'd never been born. When I wasn't wishing I'd never been born, I wished I was dead. Not once do I consider my children; what would happen to them if I weren't here? It was all about me, my hurt, my pain, my shame. Years would pass before I considered, maybe I wasn't the terrible things done and said to me as a child. Maybe I wasn't the terrible things I allowed to be done and said to me once I became a woman. Maybe I wasn't the terrible things I'd done and said to myself. Maybe…

Money! Money! Money!

So I'm back in the church doing what I "think" church members do—singing loud, clapping my hands, stomping my feet, and screaming glory hallelujah! Praise the Lord! Saying, "Thank ya, Jesus," and paying my tithes, not to honor God, what I do, I do; to honor me. I'm offering up false praise and tithing to my way to the grave. I'm holding the shovel. I'm digging the hole; I just don't have the "good sense" to know it. The preacher's holier-than-thou sermons fall on deaf ears. The same sermon Sunday after Sunday preached slightly different. Hypocrite! He ain't foolin' nobody! It's all about the money! It's more blessed to give than receive! Liar! God loves a cheerful giver! Bullcrap! Give and it will be given unto you in good measure, pressed down and overflowing! Whatever! Life dealt me a crappy hand. Life said I would never amount to anything. Life said I was nothing! Well, I'm the one holding all the cards now! Every check I put in the collection plate is a card, a card that screams, "In yo face! Look at me! I'm still here! Look at me! I am somebody! Look at all the money I'm tithing! Look at what a 'good' Christian I am! Look at me! Look at me!"

But what I'm really saying is look but don't see; hear but don't listen. Look at my beautiful, clean outer garments; don't see my ugly, filthy inner rags. Hear my convenient lies; don't listen to the inconvenient truth resonating in your ears. Look at my divine generosity; don't see your ungodly greed. I don't know when it happened; when I became the well-dressed, self-absorbed, heartless, arrogant, look-at-me Christian I despised so much as a child. But here I am, smiling the same fake smile, mouthing the same fake words, pretending I care knowing I don't. Sadly, even more years will pass before I discern I was always somebody in the eyes of God.

I grow older, but in no ways wiser. I'm flesh rich and spirit poor. I have everything I "think" I want, everything the world says I need to be happy, accepted, and content. I live in the suburbs, I drive a nice car, wear nice clothes, and make enough money to do whatever I want whenever I want. So why am I so unhappy? Why am I jumping in and out of religious denominations and doomed relationships like I'm shopping for a new pair of shoes? Protestant, Catholic, Baptist, Luthern, Jehovah's Witnesses, nondenominational, manual labor man, businessman, "one day I'm gonna be somebody" man, "can a sista help a brotha out" man. I spend a lot of time trying to make dysfunctional relationships functional, but the minute a church makes me feel uncomfortable, I'm out the door, window-shopping for a new one. Preferably one that doesn't hurt, rub, or pinch.

Finding a new church isn't the problem; getting rid of the guilt mounting inside me is the problem. The guilt I'm feeling makes no sense; what do I have to feel guilty about? Nobody ever felt guilty about me! Not the church! Not God! Not Jesus! Not my family! I don't know what's happening; there's something wrong inside of me. It doesn't feel bad. It just feels wrong. I don't know what it is or how it got there; I just want it gone! Not to mention it feels like I'm being watched. Why would anyone be watching me? I suddenly recall something I heard a pastor say about God sending His Spirit to Earth to live inside people. He called it the Holy Ghost! Could that be who's watching me? Yeah, right! God's Spirit living inside of me! No way am I acknowledging that kinda crazy!

Wouldn't a person have to be good for God's spirit to live inside them? If God's Spirit is living inside of me, why am I so messed up? Why hasn't He tried to help me? Better yet, why hasn't He tried to help Himself? He must want out of this mess as much as I do. Whatever! I wish I knew who's watching me and why. My mom used to say, "Be careful what you wish for, you just might get it." Well! Mom was right! It appears there's more to me than meets the eye, there's another me living inside of me. But that isn't what scares me most. What scares me most is she wants out! She's the one behind my feelings of guilt, the reason I toss and turn throughout the night, the constant whispering in my ear, "Nothing good will come from this life you're living."

What's she talking about? She doesn't know me and I sure as heck don't know her! Where did she come from? Has she always been inside me? What happens to me if she gets out? I decide I'm better off not knowing. Just the thought of her getting out is terrifying. Now that I know she exists, I need to stay ahead of her, take precautions, guard my emotions, anticipate her next move. Shouldn't be hard considering she's me. Talk about stuck on stupid! Inside me's intentions are crystal clear. She wants control. She wants to take over! I think she's trying to kill me! Well, I ain't having it! This is my life; this is my body! She needs to go back to wherever she came from! I try to pretend she isn't there, but it's no use; she's getting stronger. Why can't she mind her own business? Why can't she leave me alone? My life was good before she came and messed everything up. When inside me gets to moving around too much, I think about all the good things I've done, all the money I've given; all the compliments I've gotten from pastors over the years.

"Sister Taylor is an outstanding Christian! She tithes far more than ten percent, and she always gives an offering. Because of her generosity, the church is helping more people than ever! I don't know where we'd be without Sister Taylor."

Everybody says I'm a good Christian! Everybody can't be wrong! Can they? I decide its time to share all the good I'm doing with my daughter. I call her and instantly wish I hadn't. Right in the middle of telling my daughter about all the good I've done, how much I'm appreciated, and how much my students admire me; she cuts me off! No excuse me, Mom; no I'm so proud of you, Mom. If that isn't bad enough, she offers up what I'm assuming she considers to be words of wisdom. She says and I quote, "A lot of good people are going to hell, Mom."

I think to myself, *What the hell is that supposed to mean? Is she implying I'm going to hell? Who the hell does she think she is? Who the hell does she think she's talking to? Has she forgotten who I am? I'm her mother! Not her child!*

I want to crawl through the phone, wrap my hands around my daughter's throat, and wring her neck. Instead, I tell her I love her; I need to get back to work and hang up. I'm totally pissed! I can't believe my baby girl just told me I'm going to hell! She hasn't lived long enough to know what I know! She hasn't been through what I've been through. She's not God! She doesn't know where I'm going! I ain't going hell! Like I mentioned earlier, I'm getting older, but in no ways wiser. I try to shake off the soul-shaming words of my daughter but they cling to me like a skunk. Thankfully, though unbeknownst to me at the time; revelation is enroute!—Life is better whole in the Body of Christ; than broken in a broken world.

More years will pass before I acknowledge physically what I've always known spiritually. If I do end up in hell, it won't be God or Lucifer who puts me there; it will be me. God, the King of heaven, God who loves me beyond measure, can't keep me out of hell. Lucifer, the ruler of hell, Lucifer who hates, all that God loves, can't put me in hell. The honor or dishonor of where I spend eternity falls solely to me. If I end up in hell, it will be a hell of my choosing, my design, my making, and my sentencing. It will not be the physical hell I imagined in life. It isn't raging fire or smoldering ash; it's pitch-black and void, both near and far. I sense the presence of others. I cannot see them, I cannot hear them; I am alone yet not alone. I hear wailing and grinding teeth—my wailing, my teeth.

My flesh isn't burning. I have no flesh, yet my blistering soul, is fully aware. Physicality no longer exists. There is nowhere to turn, nowhere to go, nowhere to run, nowhere to hide, no choices to make, no forgiveness to ask. I yield to hell's *only truth*. It isn't a physical concept—it's a spiritual reality. The physical hell I hypothesized in life would be far kinder than the spiritual reality that awaits me in this godless place. The reality of forever knowing, forever reliving, forever remembering, forever regretting the unrepented life choices that put me here. Forever knowing all the wrong I said and did, all the right I should have said and done but chose not to. Forever remembering loved ones, forever knowing they don't remember me. Forever enduring the agony, pain, and suffering I caused. Forever knowing I did this to myself. Forever grieving; I will never again feel God's presence. Forever grieving; though no one remembers heaven; God remembers me in hell. Forever grieving; God is with me in death; as He was in life. Forever grieving; God has not forsaken me. Forever grieving; God continues to love me; in spite of…"

"I have loved you with an everlasting love." *"I will never leave nor forsake you."* Jeremiah 31:3/Hebrew 13:5

When I did bad things as a child, I got a whoopin'/whipping. Momma didn't sit me down and talk to me. She didn't ask why I did what I did. As far as mom was concerned; there wasn't anything to talk about. She simply told me to go outside and pick three long green branches from the large bush on the side of the house so she could make a switch. Having to pick the branches for my punishment was as painful as the whooping. It was like being whooped twice, first my mind then my body. When I took too long picking Mom's branches, she'd yell down at me from the upstairs window, "Girl! Stop pussyfootin' round! The longer you take pickin' those branches, the longer you gonna get whooped."

Mom's whoopin' switch couldn't be made from just any branch. The branches had to be young, long, thin, and green. Young long thin green branches, bend and wrap; old thick brown branches crack and break. Momma lines up the bottom end of the branches, ties them together with thread, places them between her knees, braids them like hair, and ties the top ends together. When she's done braiding, she swings the switch through the air to test its strength and pliability. Satisfied with the strength, pliability, and swing of her switch, momma tells me to take off my clothes. Momma didn't whoop clothes, she whooped meat. I asked her once if I could keep my clothes on. She cocked her head to the side, gave me "the" look, and said, "No." When I asked why not, she said, "Clothes just get in the way." Butt-naked, and scared, but too obstinate to show fear, I order myself not to cry, clench my fist, close my eyes and brace for the searing pain.

When I became a mother, if my kids did something wrong, they got whipped as well, more so my boys than my daughter. But never with a braided switch; I used a belt or the palm of my hand. After I obtained guardianship of my grandsons, if they did wrong, they got whipped as well, also with a belt or the palm of my hand. However, I soon realize, my grandsons are nothing like my sons were at their age. They had a whole nother mindset; often appearing incapable of grasping the Life Lesson of the Whoopin. I got a lot of whippings growing up, but I rarely got whipped for the same thing. Unlike my sons and grandsons, I learned the 1st law of the whoopin early on! Never! Ever! Repeat! Why you got whooped in the first place. Repeat whoopins were always worse. Primarily, because momma talked through the whole whoopin; often pausing between each word to make sure I felt just how pissed off she was about havin to whoop me for the same thing. "How! Many! Times! You! Gonna! Get! Whooped! For! The! Same! Thang! If! You! Don't! Care! Bout! Gettin! Whooped! Again! I Don't! Care! Bout! Whoopin! You! Again! Go! Head! Do IT again! Do IT again! Next time it's gonna be worse!" Covered in sweat, naked and bleeding, I think to myself, "It can't get, no worse than this!" Wrong! My sons frequently got two or three whippings for doing the same thing but ultimately learned from their mistakes, moved on, and found something else to get into. My grandsons got whippings for the same thing over and over and over and over yet didn't appear to learn. Once the sting of the belt wore off, they were right back at it.

I slowly began to realize it wasn't that my grandsons didn't comprehend; they simply didn't care. They were defiant. I decide to try something different; I decide to take away all their stuff as well as their privileges. I take away toys, video games, phone privileges, don't let them watch television, listen to the radio, go to their friend's house or the basketball court, and voila! They begin to understand their actions have consequences. No, they didn't turn into angels. They did, however, become less defiant and more appreciative.

My "signature hell" is sorta, kinda, like that—a forever knowing. Forever knowing the choices I made during my life were the branches I chose, painstakingly braided and tied into switches to whip myself—for eternity. Tightly braided switches, bending, twisting, wrapping consequences whipping mercilessly throughout my eternal death. Just as I took away the things my grandsons loved during their young lives, so too will I forever take away the things I loved in life; upon my eternal death. Sadly I still have a long way to go and grow. Thankfully, this hell-spun bit of knowledge is still a ways off as well. It's not that I have a problem admitting I've made bad choices; I just don't think my bad choices are as bad as those of other Christians, and I believe my monetary contributions to the church prove I'm better than most.

The more I try to convince myself I'm a good person, the harder inside me fights to get out, not only that, it feels like, she's gotten stronger. How did she get so strong so fast? I'm also starting to sense something else, another presence. Come on! There's someone else inside of me; how's that even possible?! By the time I figure out what's going on, it's too late. Yup! It's Him, the Holy Spirit! The crazy I refused to acknowledge. He's helping inside me orchestrate her escape and my surrender! Can they do that? My flesh feels weird; creepy-crawly. Why does my flesh feel creepy-crawly? I have nothin' to feel creepy-crawly about! None of this makes any sense! One minute I'm sad; the next I'm happy. One minute I'm confrontational; the next I'm welcoming. What the heck! I need to find a way to stop whatever's going on inside of me. If I don't, inside me is gonna get out! If she gets out; there'll be no pushing her back in! I don't know what this other me is! I don't know how she got inside of me! Why is she trying to get out? If I don't know what she is, how she got in, or why she's trying to get out; how do I fight her? What I do know is this; the me I've come to know—is dying. My flesh is tired but continues to fight—It/I don't want to die. I increase my tithes and offerings. Unable to sleep I start taking sleeping pills. Nothing works!

No matter how much I do, no matter how much I give, no matter how many sleeping pills I take, inside me and the Holy Spirit don't back down. My good works, monetary contributions, and lack of sleep mean nothing to them. I write bigger checks. The bigger the check, the better I feel; the better I feel, the more I give; the more I give, the more the pastors and brethren praise my generosity. I gulp down their praises like a magical elixir. The more they praise, the more I drink; the more I drink, the more I thirst; the more I thirst, the more I need man's approval. The more I need man's approval; the more money man wants in return. There appears to be no end to my need or man's greed.

Of course, I know it's all about the money! I don't care! What men do or don't do isn't my problem. They're the ones declaring themselves "men of God," the ones God called to do His work. They're not being truthful about who they are or what they're doing, so why should I? They're the "shepherds"; I'm just a member of the flock. I have no empathy, no sympathy, or anything else for the likes of lying, greedy, self-serving men. What they do or don't do is between them and God! All I care about is me! What's in it for me? I need to be encouraged. I need to be reassured. I need someone to tell me I'm a good person. If that encouragement and reassurance happens to come in the form of lies and deception, so be it! My entire life has been lies and deception! Round and round I go; where I end up, only God knows.

I need to make more money to fix me, more money for people to like me, more money for people to respect me, more money to like and respect myself, more money to be happy, more money to be less sad, more money to forget the bad, more money to pretend the good. But money doesn't do any of those things; it doesn't know how. It's currency, dead painted faces, numbers, and words printed in ink, it's heartless, soulless, and loveless. Manmade paper and coins cosigned with gold, having no redeeming qualities: *In God We Trust.* But, do we trust Him? Human indicators say we don't.

I'm slowly starting to realize inside me wants me to see what outside me, my flesh, wants to keep hidden; that my freedom is an illusion, that I am both prisoner and jailer, that I merely moved from the prison cell of the impoverished into the prison cell of the middle class. Beautiful and alive on the outside, ugly and doomed on the inside. Unresolved conflicts, anger, bitterness, shame, and unforgiveness have laid claim to my soul; they anticipate the moment they can finish what they started in me as a child.

I blamed lack for my problems. Lack was the reason evil took notice of me. Lack was the reason Daddy abandoned me. Lack was the reason my momma always cried. Lack was the reason nobody loved me. Lack was the reason nobody cared what happened to me. Lack was the reason I was taken from my bed night after night. Lack was the reason no matter how much I cried, no matter how hard I tried, no matter how good I was, no matter how much I prayed, nothing changed. I couldn't wait to grow up and make money. I thought money would make everything better, but it didn't; it only made things "appear" better. All the problems I thought money would solve multiplied. Not because of money, because of my love of money. It occurs to me, what if money isn't the problem. What if I'm the problem? Evil whispers to me in a soothing voice, "You've been through so much. You worked hard for what you have. You deserve this. It's high time something good happened for you! You deserve to be happy! You deserve to enjoy life! Why, should you change? No one ever changed for you! No one helped you! Stay where you are; just a little while longer. No need to rush. No need to change just yet."

I should have run for my life, but I didn't. Instead, I listened, I agreed. I stayed. I agreed because evil told me what I wanted to hear. I agreed because he gave me, permission, to excuse my wrongs, permission to hate, permission to be angry, permission to take my hate and anger out on others, permission to avenge myself. Evil knows my fears, he knows because he introduced me to fear when I was six-years-old. But evil didn't put me on the love of money path, I did that all by myself. Money didn't put itself in the church collection plate, I did. Money didn't place itself above others, I did. Money didn't splurge itself on needless wanton things, I did. Money didn't brag or boast, I did. Money wasn't proud or arrogant, I was. Money is inanimate, it doesn't care how it's used or who uses it. God, on the other hand, does. In due time, He will take the money I fraudulently sowed and use it for good.

Many things are revealed to me during this disingenuous period of my life, but the most troubling revelation—spirits recognize themselves in others, which caused me to pause and ponder, *What did spirits recognize in me?* I'm angry, self-absorbed, and unforgiving, pardoned within—condemned without. Broken and confused, Humpty Dumpty sitting on a wall not of my making yet now of my choosing. Constantly falling, repeatedly breaking, unable to put myself back together, unwilling to admit the severity of my brokenness, unwilling to ask for help. I conclude broken is all I'll ever be. Broken is all I'm meant to be. Broken is all I deserve to be.

Jesus revealed the possibility of me to me when I was younger. I didn't want anything to do with her; she's the one He loved not me. I could never be her; she was unsustainable. I didn't much care for the woman I was, but she's the woman I know; she's sustainable. I know what to expect and what not to expect from her. Yes, she's unhappy, but her unhappiness is familiar, even comforting at times. I'm secure in her insecurity. The woman Jesus showed me required time, effort, dedication, discipline, and sacrifice—none of which I was prepared to give. She's the church Jesus was referring to when He said, "Upon this rock I will build My church."

She's a member of His body. She's in His service 24 hours a day, 7 days a week, 365 1/4 days a year. No way was I willing, ready, or anywhere near able to commit to something like that. Being a member of man's church, attending once a week, on religious holidays, and sporadically showing up for various church functions, shouting "Glory, glory! Hallelujah! Praise the Lord! God is good all the time!" Clapping my hands and stomping my feet was more my speed. Man's church gave me six days of freedom to do whatever I wanted to do; the Church of Christ wanted my total commitment seven days a week. No time off! No excuses! Where's the fun in that?

When I feel inside me getting close to the surface, I whip out my checkbook: Mo-money! Mo-money! Mo-money! I'm tithing my way to salvation, writing off the salvation Jesus suffered and died for with a ballpoint pen and a thin piece of colored paper. Talk about stuck on stupid! It don't get *no* stupider than that! After more years than I care to admit, my spirit/inside me conquers my flesh. Tired and weary, my flesh surrenders to my spirit and the Spirit of God within me.

It took a pimp, two child molesters, an abusive husband, three subsequent dysfunctional relationships, the drug addiction of my youngest son, the drug addiction of his girlfriend (the mother of his three sons), obtaining legal guardianship of their children, taking in my grandsons younger sister, and losing my high-paying job for me to finally cry out to Jesus, but cry out to Him I did! And despite all I'd done, despite all I'd said, He answered my cry. At that moment, I stopped pretending; at that moment, I knew. When it comes to God, there's no lukewarm, no in-between, no straddling the fence. I'm either in or out, inside with Jesus or outside in the world. Once again I'm given a choice: continue my toxic relationship with the world or be in a devoted relationship with Christ. Continue dying in the world or start living in Christ. This time, I choose correctly; this time, I choose Christ Jesus. So imagine my disappointment when things don't instantly change. Bills still aren't getting paid, and I'm eating whatever food my grandkids leave on their plates. Sound familiar? Things go from bad to worse when my minivan gets repossessed! Talk about déjà vu!

I eventually get a job substitute teaching. It's an on-call position, which means I only work if someone calls in sick, takes the day off, or goes on vacation. I'm barely making enough money to pay the rent, let alone pay all the other bills and buy food. And because my minivan got repossessed, I no longer had a way to get back and forth to work. I didn't know what I was going to do. I didn't know what God was doing or why. Then one day the miraculous happened. Mr. and Mrs. Frankland, a "white" couple around my age, who lived a few houses down from us, knocked on my front door and handed me a set of car keys. I kid you not! They brought me a car! Who does that?!—God does that!

The Franklands giving me a car was the most amazing, kindest thing anyone's ever done for me. Other than that; my life was a repeat of raising my three kids; plus one. When my grandchildren came to live with me, I still had my high-paying job. I brought them all new clothes. I traded in my cool car for a minivan and moved them out of Detroit into suburbs. No drive-by shooting, no drunks or addicts laundering outside the neighborhood convenience store, no drug dealers selling their poison on the street corners; no wailing police sirens throughout the night. Everything costs way more in the suburbs, but knowing my grandchildren are safe and will get the education they deserve is well worth the cost. Besides, I made more than enough money to support them. The thought of ever losing my job never crossed my mind. But here I sit, knee-deep in bills again, earning less than a third of what I made as a sales rep with five times the financial responsibility. Why would God give me the responsibility of four kids and not give me the financial means to care for them?

One of the *not*-so-feel-good things I've experienced about God over the years, when I conveniently forget; He inconveniently reminds. Which is exactly what He does when I'm forced to take a second job. God has a funny "not so funny" sense of humor. My second job has multiple duties—food preparer, food server, cashier, dishwasher, and occasional window washer. No college degree required. Yep, there I was again, doing exactly what I swore I'd never do again—serving food, wiping down tables, sweeping floors, and cleaning up after people. Arby's Restaurant is no Chuck Muir's, but it's got way better food benefits. Not only can I confiscate refused orders, I can have whatever food hasn't sold by close of business. I work last shift, so there's usually lots of unsold food. And voila! Just like that, our food problem is solved. My grandkids love Arby's sandwiches and sticky buns. Some nights they wait up for me to see what goodies I brought home. Praise the Lord! No more late-night cold tater-totes! Sadly, my joy is short-lived. My substitute teaching assignments dwindle to almost nothing, and I have to find a second, second job! I scream out, at the top of my voice, "Enough! Already! What do You want from me? Just tell me so I can do it! I can't keep living like this! Why did You give me these kids; when you knew I wouldn't be able to take care of them? I did what you asked. What more do you want?"

Suddenly, just like that day in my bedroom closet when I was eight years old. Suddenly, just like that day in church when I was introduced to the woman I could be but declined, there He stood! Jesus! Arms wide open! No anger. No condemnation. No it's about time. No what took you so long? Nothing but love! I fall to my knees; at that moment, in His Presence, I know we're going to be okay. At that moment, in His Presence, I stop wondering why; I stop asking when. I stop being afraid. At that moment, in His Presence, for the first time in my life, I stop worrying about my life. I know what's expected of me. I know what it means to know that He is God. To be at peace; to be still. From that day till this, when bills come, I lay them down, look up and say, "God, You got mail."

Jehovah-Jireh, God Jehovah will provide.

Shortly thereafter, my eldest son and my daughter offered their financial assistance. I did not ask; they offered. Money starts coming in from other sources as well. People are sending money through the mail. When I ask them why, they say they were led to. Money I didn't deposit shows up in my bank account. Thinking someone made a mistake, I leave it there for a few days. I receive three hundred dollars through the mail inside a card. The enveloped isn't sealed; the money could have fallen out; someone could have taken it! Zero probability of that happening! What God puts in motion stays in motion until it arrives at its appointed destination.

Lord knows I've come a long way since then. The Lord also knows I still have a long way to go. For as long as I live, I will still have a long way to go. My final destination will not be reached in this lifetime nor upon this earth. Each new day is a new beginning, a new opportunity to do good, to right wrongs, ask forgiveness, offer forgiveness, or be forgiven. Each morning I wake up closer to God than the day before. Each new day is a joy to behold. God knew every choice I'd make before I made it. He knew every lie I'd speak before I spoke it. He knew every broken promise I'd break before I broke it. God knew my sin-nature before He created me yet still deemed me deserving of creation; deserving of His Sacrifice, deserving of His

Son, deserving of His Holy Spirit; His Love, Forgiveness, Grace, and Mercy. He deemed me—deserving of you.

God knew I needed time to reach the end of me; only at the end of me would I find Him. Only at the end of me could I become the church Christ built upon a rock. Only at the end of me do I find you! Only at the end of me do I realize nothing I have belongs to me—not my family, not my children, my grandchildren, my subsequent great-grandchildren, my friends or my enemies. No one belongs to me. Nothing belongs to me. Not even me! Every breath I take is a gift from God. Only my free will/choices are my own. When Jesus ramsoned Himself, He paid the price; God gave me to Him. At the end of me, my eyes are open. I look, I see. My ears are open. I hear, I listen, not what I want to see and hear but what I need to see and hear; that there is no partiality in God. To live my life according to Him, reflective of Christ Jesus, relevant to the Holy Spirit, there can be no partiality in me.

We, humans, are unpredictable. We can be loving and kind on Monday and fit to be tied on Tuesday. Weather, traffic, bills, good hair day, bad hair day, day of the week, time of day, and etcetera dictate there is no way of knowing what we will or won't do, will or won't say, on any given day. That being said, never say never; hope and pray for the best.

Some years back, certain individuals within my family said some hurtful, untrue things about me; this continued for several years. I was so hurt. I racked my brain trying to figure out what I could have said or done to make them say so many hurtful, untrue things. The more I hurt, the more they talked; the more they talked, the more I hurt. Why? To this day, only God knows. But, when you think about it—only God knows is sufficient. Jesus suffered and died defending us; defeating every suffering, vindictive word, and deed.

"And after you have suffered a little while, the God of all grace, who has called you to his eternal glory in Christ, will himself restore, confirm, strengthen, and establish you." 1 Peter 5:10

"No weapon that is formed against thee shall prosper, and every tongue that shall rise against thee in judgment thou shalt condemn. This

is the heritage of the servants of the LORD, and their righteousness is of me, saith the LORD." Proverbs 8:19

WISDOM IN A CAN

One day, when I was feeling particularly sorry for myself, God directed me to the kitchen. Once there, He asked me to take a can of canned vegetables from the cabinet and turn it bottom-side up. The following is the canned vegetable conversation God and I had on that fateful day. He did most of the talking.

"What do you see Toni?"

"The expiration date."

"What happens if you eat these vegetables after the expiration date?"

"I get sick"

"The same holds true when you consume and meditate on negative things; you get sick. Expired food poisons and depletes the body. Negative words and deeds produce negative emotions. Negative emotions poison and diminish the mind, soul, and spirit. As long as there is breath in you, you are going to get angry; you are going to be hurt; you are going to be disappointed. As long as there is breath in you; you choose how you respond to negative words and deeds. Even the most righteous have been driven to anger, hurt, and despair. Just as this can of vegetables has a shelf-life/expiration date; so too must negative emotions. You have authority over your surroundings. You choose how the words and actions of others affect you and for how long.

I must have looked, totally confused, or totally stupid. Because God paused. But not for long.

Your choices shape your surroundings; emotionally, spiritually, and physically. Right now, you're angry. You're hurt. You feel betrayed. What you decide to do with that anger, hurt, and sense of betrayal is up to you; not the person who caused it. How much of your life/time, are you prepared to give your anger/hurt feelings? Seconds, minutes, hours, days, weeks, months; years? Forgiveness is the "only" answer to negative things. Even when it doesn't feel fair—forgive. After you forgive assign your negative emotions a measure of time; a shelf-life/expiration date. Will you always be successful? No, you will not. However, in due time, you will notice; the more you forgive the easier it's becoming. Little by little, forgiving becomes as breathing; in and out. Less and less of your life/time is spent on negative things. You're happy. You're at peace. You breathe easy."

"The Spirit of God has made me, and the breath of the Almighty gives me life." Job 33:4

"As long as my breath is still within me and the breath of God remains in my nostrils" Job 27:3

I'm so grateful to God; grateful for all He's shown and taught me. But, on that fateful day, four words rose above the rest. Four words that would change my life forever. "Give them to Me."

"Give who to You?" I ask.

"Everyone," he answers. "Let there be no more yours or theirs, younger or older, higher or lower, more or less, better or worse, you versus them."

"Okay," I reply.

Right then and there I gave God back what was His. My first return—me. Next, my mom and dad, followed by my brother, sisters, grandmothers, and extended family. Next up, my children, grandchildren, unborn child, ex-husband, ex-lovers, in-laws, friends, and enemies. Only after returning God's children to their Creator do I regain the power and authority I so foolishly threw away. Only after returning what was never mine, to begin with, do I discern my recklessness; charging head-on into battles; not mine to fight or win. Every hurt, betrayal, and disappointment, fueling my anger; excusing my impropriety.

Burdens lifted eyes-wide-open I take a sober; impartial look within. There, in the midst, of my life's trials and tribulations, I see my soul salvation. Two words; eleven letters—FREE! FORGIVE! According to scripture the number 11 symbolizes; disorder, chaos, and judgment. For me to rid myself of disorder and chaos; that I might receive favorable judgment I needed to forgive and free. Forgive my enemies; the living and the dead. Forgive the hurt, pain, and shame. Free the prisoners locked inside my soul. But, as with most things in life, there's a catch. In my case that catch was me!

From the exceptional to the mundane, the most valuable to the least valuable; the largest to the smallest; the visible to the hidden, the most joyful to the most sorrowful, God's divine plan for our life confers. From our beginning until our end; everything about us is important to God. Everything God has done, is doing, and will do, is perfect, decent, in order; compassionate, and thoughtful. Notwithstanding, all the awful things we've done and said, we remain beautiful in God's eyes. *"You are altogether beautiful, my love; there is no flaw in you."* Song of Solomon 4:7

The Catch: God bought me face to face with me—I couldn't forgive my enemies until I forgave myself. I couldn't forgive the hurt, pain, and shame inflicted on me by others until I forgave the hurt, pain, and shame inflicted on me; by me. I couldn't resolve my distrust of others until I resolved my distrust of myself. I couldn't set my prisoners free until I set myself free. God's perfect timing; God's perfect order. God's perfect plan.

Only after confessing my crimes against myself was I freed; from myself. Only after freeing me from me was I free to align with God's plan for my life. Only after I aligned with God's plan, does God do, what only God can!—He restores the brokenness. The brokenness caused by others; the brokenness caused by me. I lived so much of my life on the run, scared, ashamed, angry, and blind; looking every which-away but the Way! I never saw Love coming! But He came and got me anyway. I was blind, but now I see. I was deaf, but now I hear. I take my life out of my hands and place it into His.

*****

Remember the number 11; it will come up again later. Remember what it symbolizes; disorder, chaos, and judgment.

The day I gave God back what was His; His impartiality washes over me, and I discern; there is no such thing as loving one person more than another. I can't love my child more than someone else's child. However, I can say with a fair degree of certainty, carrying a child for nine months, giving birth to him/her, nurturing and watching them grow gives rise to a mother's love, not more love, not better love, a physical, spiritually connected love. A spiritual connection, between mother, and child, that remains intact, long after the umbilical cord is severed. Love is universal, unrestricted, and unchanging. It doesn't change form from one person to the next. It doesn't come with a human pedigree. It doesn't adhere to human frailties. It doesn't have preferences. It doesn't come in multiple shapes, sizes, or colors. Love is God; God is love. It/He cannot be added to nor can It/He be subtracted from. Worldly love is conditional; it says there are those of us who deserve to be loved and those of us who don't deserve to be loved. Worldly love can be measured and counted; it is tentatively given and harshly taken away.

The world offers hate disguised as love. Lies disguised as truth. Defeat disguised as victory. Ugliness disguised as beauty. Wrong disguised as right. Death disguised as life. It tells us we can measure what God says cannot be measured. We can count what God says cannot be counted. We can take what God says isn't ours to take. The world gives. The world takes away. Without care. Without reason. Without cause. Without explanation. It is obligated to nothing, empathetic to no one. It never forgives; it never forgets. To love as God loves, I had to disavow worldly love. The first step towards doing that was to give the world, and everything affiliated with it, back to God.

I've had a lot of "best day ever!—God days over the years. But my bestest, best day ever!—God day! Was the day I gave myself, everybody, and everything back to God. On that day, Grace taught me to breathe; Mercy taught me to see and listen. On that day, I realized, everyone in my life was God assigned or God allowed. They don't belong to me. I don't belong to them. We belong to God. Everyone God assigns or allows in my life is there for a season and a specific reason. I don't always agree with or understand the reasonings and allowances of God. Pretty sure, that's what, Isaiah 55:8-9 is referring to… *"For my thoughts are not your thoughts, neither are your ways my ways. For as the heavens are higher than the earth, so are my ways higher than your ways and my thoughts your thoughts."* Thing is, I don't have to agree with or understand why God assigns or allows, to know, everyone/everything He assigns or allows is for my good; according to His Good Purpose for my life. As opposed to my often-times self-destructive "purposes".

The day I gave everyone back to God my whole world changed. The heaviness of shame, anger, hurt, and disappointment falls away. I take my first breath on earth as an adult. I see and listen for the first time. I am one with humanity. No longer crippled by anger and unforgiveness I discern; forgiving *"the children of God"* is waaaaaay easier!—than forgiving the parents, grandparents, children, grand-children, siblings, family, friends, and enemies of Toni. That, good, bad, right, wrong, or indifferent God is "our" Father. God is "our" judge. We are not equipped to judge one another.

God's words circle-back—compassion resounds throughout my being. I listen with new ears. *"Give them to Me."* I see with new eyes. *"God's amazing grace."* I feel with new emotion *"The inconceivable depths of God's unconditional love."* In that ear-resounding, eye-open-ing, soul-cleansing, heart-pounding moment; I hear, I see, I feel, the overwhelming, unrelenting compassion of my Father's words, *"Give them to Me."* Not only was He offering to take my burdens upon Himself; He was asking my permission—*to heal me!*

Toni Taylor felt unloved, unappreciated, unaccepted, and disre-spected. She looked to others for love, happiness, and accreditation. But no matter how hard she tried, no matter how much she did for others, she couldn't overcome her feelings of abandonment and betrayal. The day Toni Taylor gave God back what was His, she was finally able to breathe, finally able to let go, finally able to escape the trappings of her flesh and embrace the wrappings of her spirit, finally able to stand down, finally able to let Moses Esther step up and take her rightful place, finally able and willing to embrace Moses Esther's forgiving spirit, insight, confidence, empathy, understanding, and strength. Where Toni Taylor ended, Moses Esther began. Together they would accomplish what Toni Taylor was told, she was incapable of doing. Now whole and complete I know—I am not a mistake! God doesn't make mistakes! I am by His design! I am, who He cre-ated me to be. I am, who I was born to be. I am, Toni Moses Esther

Taylor! I am, the daughter of God Jehovah!! Today, what was lost, broken, and stolen is returned and restored! Today, God renewed His purposeful plan as decreed—Saturday, February 19, 1949. My earth-birth-day.

It is written, "The battle is not yours, but the Lord's." I take this to mean all battles big and small, biological, societal, manmade, and self-made. I also take this to mean, though the battle rages on, the war is already won!

The day I gave God back what was His, suddenly I see, suddenly I hear, suddenly I feel the whole of us, not just my tiny biological piece. I see us as we were created to be seen. I see us through the impartial eyes of God; not the partial eyes of man. Living my life according to God, reflective of Christ Jesus under the tutelage and guidance of the Holy Spirit, beyond the scope of human biology, physiology, worldly influences, societal norms, and biological family assumptions, has grown, enriched, and empowered me in a way I can only describe as whole and complete. Within that wholly-completeness; nothing is missing—I am absolute. There is no doubt. There is no uncertainty. My absolute in knowing God is well able. My absolute in knowing God's grace and tender mercies are made new every day. My absolute in knowing God moves within me, around me, and through me. Through Him, I am well able. My absolute in knowing God makes all things possible; without Him, nothing is probable. I pray what you have read thus far offers some degree of solace. My soul/sole purpose is the unification of we the people. We God's people.

Why I Wrote This Book

I wrote this book because God asked me to. God and I have an amazing relationship, but we don't always see eye to eye, which was the case; February 19, 2017, my 68th birthday. I have been delivering messages and writing letters to people as God directs for more than twenty years. In all that time He never asked me to write anything like this. I declined His request and proceeded to tell Him why. I didn't want to worry my kids. Some of my family members and dearest friends had voted for Mr. Trump. Lastly, I didn't want to write a book about prejudice and hate. But truth be told, it wasn't any of those things.

In order for me to write what God wanted as He wanted, I would have to dig up my past, unearth dead people and dead things I preferred remain dead and buried. Done talking, and explaining I waited for God to respond—nothing. I thought to myself good, glad that was over. I honestly thought the matter was closed; I was wrong. On February 19, 2018, at 4:45 a.m., eastern standard time, my 69th birthday, God woke me with the following words, "You are My first choice. You are not My only choice."

No shouting, no threats, no warnings, no flashes of light, no rumblings of thunder. His voice was clear, calm, and matter-of-fact. Do it, don't do it, my choice. God and I have been talking long enough for me to know when He's disappointed; I can feel it. But that day was different. What I felt wasn't disappointment; it was sadness. Knowing I caused God's sadness totally freaked me out! But knowing He had a ram in the bush waiting to take my place freaked me out even more. This book was going to be written with me or without me. But grace was on my side. God knew I would refuse Him long before He asked me. Everything God asks of us comes with a perfect measure of redeeming grace. The time and season of this book were determined eons ago. On February 19, 2018, God gave me a second chance to be its author.

By this time, I'd been watching and listening to President Trump for two years. February 19, 2019, my 70th birthday, God instructs me to stop watching, listening to, or reading anything having to do with President Trump; should his name come up in conversation I am to excuse myself and walk away. He also tells me all written references, to the past must be relevant, to the present, and all writing must stop by noon, February 19, 2020. When, I asked Him why? He said anything written after that date and time would be written in anger; with bias. February 19, 2020, my 71st birthday, twelve-noon, I stop writing and upload, American, Donald Trump, God, and Me— Through My Great-Grandma Eyes to my publicist.

I was slowly starting to understand why God chose me to write this book. Why He asked me to travel back through time. Why He asked me to expose my past to strangers; write about things I kept hidden from my children, family, and friends for years. The thought of resubjecting myself to all that hurt, pain, and shame was agonizing, but the thought of further saddening God was unimaginable. Uncertain of what I might say, I bit down on my lower lip as hard as I could, without drawing blood, and remained still. I don't recall ever sitting that still before, if ever. It was at that moment God revealed, ever so gently, dark things exposed by the light are powerless. The shared hurt of a single individual can ease the hurt of thousands. From a single speck of ash, endless fields of beauty bloom.

God was asking me to resurrect the dead to help the living. He was asking me to write it all down. Write down how those with power and authority used their power and authority to rape, abuse, and shame me—without fear of the consequences. How those who could have stopped the abuse chose to remain silent for personal gain. Ugly, painful, shameful things laid the foundation for this book, but God's prevailing good, my restoration and recommence, wrote the pages. I believe writing this book is a portion of the latter years' happiness Christ promised me when I was a child. This is my life, thus far. This is my past, present, and in-between, working together for good. For there is no evil greater than God prevailing good.

I watched and listened to President Trump for three years; during that time, despite how hard I tried not to become emotionally involved, there was simply no getting around the awful things he implied, said, and did. Everything about him—his tone of voice, his mannerisms, his constant bragging and boosting—inched my past closer to my present. Everything about him screamed, "Do you recognize me? Do you remember me?"

I remember thinking how was I supposed to write a book about my past, reflective of my present, if just thinking about Mr. Trump made me anxious? The more I thought about digging up the past, the more apprehensive I became, but apprehensive or not I needed to get myself together! God had given me a second chance, I wasn't about to blow it because I was afraid of the past. Time to put on my big girl panties and dive in! Past, be dammed! So much easier said than done. God said my words had to be written with conscientious compassion and careful observation. What I heard was, "Walk through the exploding minefields of your war-torn past with care and compassion!" Really? Upset; wanting to speak, but knowing my response would, most definitely result in me saying something really, really stupid, I kept my mouth shut and nodded my head when appropriate. Little doubt on my part, God knew exactly what I was thinking.

Over the course of the next six months, I wrote nonstop, not once did God asks me, what I'd written. I took His silence to mean He was pleased. Wrong! Mid-August 2019, God asked me to read what I'd written. I did and instantly wish I hadn't. The ugly, bitter, angry, hateful words glaring back at me from the computer monitor caused me to hang my head in shame. Though I didn't relish writing about my past, I honestly thought I had moved on! I couldn't have been more wrong! How could I feel this way and not know it? More importantly, how could I still feel this way and have sincerely served God all these years? I had no idea I was still this messed up, but God did. How could He trust me to reach out to others on His behalf knowing I felt this way? I was so messed up I didn't know what to do. God knew how messed up I was but never said a word. Needless to say, it took a minute; and by minute, I mean days to get past the shame and disappointment of what I uncovered about myself. I thought my past was dead and buried; it wasn't. It was hibernating, waiting for me to return.

There's a lot to be said for God knowing everything—every thought, word, and deed—before, during, and after it's considered spoken and/or carried out. First and foremost, no matter how many times we mess up, no matter how many bad choices we make, He never gives up on us. Anyway, once I finally got over feeling sorry for myself, God said, "Read it again, then delete it and start over."

What God said about me writing with conscientious compassion and careful observation resonated within me. It appeared I didn't have a problem writing with conscientious compassion and careful observation when it came to others, primarily strangers. But when it came to writing with compassion and care regarding myself, those persons and things from my past, I most definitely had a problem. I silently thought to myself, *If I get through this, it's gonna wreck me.*

But God knew me better than I knew myself. He knew the bitter ugly words I wrote were residual from my childhood. He also knew whereas Toni Taylor was unable, Moses Esther was well able. She had the wherewithal to push the residual aside, the capability to write and observe, with care and compassion; beyond the painful residual of our past. She had broad shoulders, the strength to endure the remembrances of the past and the realities of the present. There was a check, in my spirit: Trust in who you are without regard to who you were. Moses Esther had no association with the flesh. She was resilient, focused, and steadfast. She would not be distracted, misled, persuaded, nor dissuaded, not by the present nor the past. My spirit will do what my flesh could not.

God asked me to think back to the day I first heard Mr. Trump speak as a presidential candidate, and I cringed, it was a day I'd just as soon forget, I heard God say, "Write it all down, Toni, add nothing. Take away nothing."

That day bolts to the forefront of my mind. I was sitting on my recliner in the living room, sipping my morning coffee. But before

I get into the troubling details of the day, I want to say this upfront: I believe God designed us multipurposed to do multiple, purposeful things during our life on earth. I believe these purposeful things were purposed to strengthen, define, enrich, and complete us; that we might in turn help strengthen, define, enrich, and complete one another. I believe writing this is one of the purposeful things God purposed me to do.

*****

Different yet the same

Physically speaking, in accordance with the world, other than both being human, President Trump and I have very little in common. He's a resident of America and the commander in chief of the United States; I'm a resident of America and the matriarch of my family. He's a Caucasian American male who grew up in luxury; I'm an African American female who grew up in poverty. He has a bachelor's degree in economics; I have a bachelor's degree in journalism. He has a sales background in business I have a sales background in postsecondary education. He's known to many; I'm known to few. He's vociferous; I'm stilled. There is partiality in him; there is no partiality in me. He was born Friday, June 14, 1946; I was born Saturday, February 19, 1949.

Spiritually speaking, in accordance with biblical scripture, President Trump and I have a lot in common. We were both created by God. We're both temporary residents of Earth, but our primary citizenship is in heaven. We were both born on the Sabbath, the only day sanctified, the Holy Day of rest, from Friday sunset until Saturday sunset. Three years and eight months separate our birthdates. When President Trump was three years old, my mom was eight months pregnant with me. In accordance, with scripture, the numbers 3 and 8 are deemed very important. The number 3 symbolizes divine wholeness, completion, and perfection; the number 8 symbolizes resurrection, regeneration, and a new beginning.

Also, in accordance, with scripture, the number 14, President Trump's birth-day, denotes a double measure of spiritual perfection. The number 19, my birth-day denotes God's perfect order, in regard, to His judgment. President Trump was born in June; the sixth month of the year. According to scripture, 6 symbolizes man and human weakness. I was born in February; the second month of the year. According to scripture, 2 symbolizes unity and harmony. 3 months separate the month of February, and the month of June. The number 3 also symbolizes God's presence and completion.

The Spiritual Preponderance of 3…

According to scripture, Christs' was 30-years-old when He began his ministry; it lasted 3 years. The number 30 symbolizes dedication to a particular task or calling. Biblically speaking; by age 30 a person has reached both physical and mental maturity, and therefore capable of handling major responsibilities.

Jesus prayed in the Garden of Gethsemane 3-times; before He was arrested. He was 33 when we nailed Him to the cross; at the 3rd hour/9 am. He suffered on the cross for 3 hours; from the 6th hour until the 9th hour. Darkness covered the earth for 3 hours. Jesus died shortly after 3 pm. The number 6; man, and human weakness. The number 9 Divine Completeness/Finality. Christ was dead 72 hours; 3 complete days and 3 complete nights. He was resurrected on the 3rd day just after sunrise. 7–2–3; the number of hours, days, and nights Jesus was dead. According to scripture, 7 symbolizes the foundation of God's word; completion and perfection; 2 symbolizes unity and harmony; 3 symbolizes harmony and completeness. Christ died at age 33; according to scripture the number 33 is linked to "certain" promises made by God. In accordance, with scripture, God made 8,810 promises; 7,487 of those promises were made to us/human-kind. My take on the aforementioned—Jesus had to die at age 33 so certain promises made by God to us/humankind could be fulfilled. Christ had to empty Himself that we might become full!…

*****

"Have this mind among yourselves, which is yours in Christ Jesus, who, though he was in the form of God, did not count equality with God a thing to be grasped, but emptied himself, by taking the form of a servant, being born in the likeness of men. And being found in human form, he humbled himself by becoming obedient to the point of death, even death on a cross." Philippians 2:5–8

When we add, 7-2-3, the 72 hours and 3 days/nights Jesus was dead, they equal 12. In accordance, with scripture, 12 is one of several numbers deemed perfect; it symbolizes God's power and authority; serves as a perfect governmental foundation, and epitomizes completion.

My take on the number 12…

God is all-powerful. All authority belongs
to God. God governs all things!

"I form light and create darkness; I make well-being and create calamity; I am the Lord, who does all these things. "Shower, O heavens, from above, and let the clouds rain down righteousness; let the earth open, that salvation and righteousness may bear fruit; let the earth cause them both to sprout; I the Lord have created it. Woe to him who strives with him who formed him, a pot among earthen pots! Does the clay say to him who forms it, 'What are you making?' or 'Your work has no handles" Isaiah 45:7–9

"The dice are cast into the lap; all decisions are from the Lord." Proverbs 16:33

In other words: We make our own decisions, but
the Lord alone determines what happens.

God could have stopped His Son's suffering; if He wanted to. God could have stopped His Son from being crucified; if He wanted to. God could have removed His Son from the cross and taken Him back to the Kingdom of Heaven; if He so chose. Better yet, by His Power, Authority, and Perfect Governing, God didn't have to send His Son to earth. Christ didn't have to be born of a woman. Christ Jesus didn't have to live as a human. Jesus didn't have to start a ministry. Jesus didn't have to preach the gospel, heal the sick, raise the dead, be lied on, flogged, mocked, spat on, nailed to a cross, suffer on a cross, die on a cross, be resurrected from the dead, ascend to heaven, or send the Holy Spirit to earth! Right? WRONG!!!! Christ's birth, life, suffering, crucifixion, death, resurrection, and ascension are our—Absolution! Absolution from our sins then. Absolution from our sins now. Absolution from our sins against, the Father, the Son, the Holy Spirit, and one another.

God's promises are guaranteed for eternity. His promises cannot be broken. Why? Because God cannot lie. No matter what we do. No matter what we say. No matter how much pain, suffering, death, and devastation we cause, God's promises are "fixed" they cannot be changed; they cannot be canceled. *"For no matter how many promises God made they are "Yes" in Christ. And through Him our "Amen" is spoken to the glory of God."* 2 Corinthians 1:20.

Being that the number 8 symbolizes a new beginning I've listed 8 of the 7,487 promises God made to us. Promises, Christ allowed himself to be disrespected, tortured, crucified, and died for at 33 years of age.

From God to us…

1. I promise to love you unconditionally
2. I promise to never leave or forsake you
3. I promise to supply all of your needs.
4. I promise My grace is sufficient
5. I promise to deliver you from your enemies
6. I promise you will not walk a road I've not already walked

7. I promise you will not be tempted or tested beyond what you can bear
8. I promise My plan for your life is to prosper you, not harm you

Quick recap: Christ was 30-years-old when He started His ministry. His ministry lasted 3 years. He was 33-years-old when we nailed Him to the cross at the 3rd hour. He suffered on the cross for 3 hours. He died at the 3rd hour. Darkness covered the earth for 3 hours. He was resurrected on the 3rd day. The number 33 is linked to "certain" promises God made to us. Those "certain" promises were made to us; this present generation—before we were even born! God created us knowing He would ransom His Son for us; that we; His children might live and not die; knowing that we; His children would torture and murder His only Begotten Son; knowing His only Begotten Son would surrender Himself unto death so we; His children could be redeemed; knowing He would turn away when His only Begotten Son cried out to Him from the cross…

"Eloi Eloi lama sabachthani?"

"My God, my God, why hast thou forsaken me?"

*****

Who does that? Oh! That would be God!

We brothers and sisters are justified in Christ! We are physical proof of the Spiritual Preponderance of 3.

In my opinion; everything went according to plan…

The ransom sacrifice of God the Father; the willing unto death sacrifice of Christ the Son, and the willing relocation, from the

Kingdom of Heaven to earth sacrifice of the Holy Spirit; were the 3 Sacrificial Acts required to guarantee our salvation.

"God presented Christ as a sacrifice of atonement, through the shedding of his blood—to be received by faith. He did this to demonstrate his righteousness because in his forbearance he had left the sins committed beforehand unpunished." Romans 3:25

In accordance, with biblical Aramaic, President Trump's birth-year, 1946, means to hook, go up, come, walk, be brought caus-atively, to bring, to bring again. Also, in accordance, with biblical Aramaic my birth-year, 1949 means to lay hold of, ring again, make a great noise, roar, discomfit, be moved, to stir, to show disquietude. What did these scriptural, and Aramaic numbers tell me? They told me, President Trump, and I were given certain spiritual gifts; that he and I were authored and designed for such a time as this to accomplish specific things; during a specific season. Yet amid my numerical revelation, I am reminded, God gave us free will. We choose how we live our lives. We choose how we use our gifts. We choose, good. We choose, evil.

Though President Trump and I have different biological parents, we have the same Heavenly Father. Our Father's name is, God Jehovah; we were both created in His image. It is by our Father's authority that we are made equal, by His authority that we are made whole, by His authority that we are joint heirs with His only Begotten Son, Christ Jesus. So what does that mean exactly? It means President Trump is my brother; it means I don't have to like what my brother says or does to love him any more than our Father, God Jehovah, has to like what I say or do to love me. Which brings me to this unde-niable truth: my life and that of President Trump was intentionally purposefully joined eons before our physical birth for such a time as this. To every thing, there is a season and a time to every purpose under the heaven.

It is because our Father, God Jehovah, created us conjointly equal, whole, and according to His image that I know this. Racism, hatred, prejudice, callousness, greed, abuse, and indifference aren't born; they're purposely bred, cultivated, and groomed. It is because

I know these things, that I grieve and pray. I grieve for the gentle boy my brother wasn't allowed to be. I grieve for the considerate teenager my brother was forbidden to be. I grieve for the kind man my brother could have been. I grieve the loss of the loving, generous, compassionate man God created my brother to be, but the world will never know. And hence, I pray. I pray for the brother I never knew. I pray for the callous man the world encouraged him to become. I pray for the bias braggart he chose to become. I pray for the inhumane man he continues to be. I pray for the day he comes face-to-face with the man our Father authored, designed and created him to be. That on that day, he sheds the flesh of the man he was raised to be, the man he chose to be, and the man society encouraged him to be. It is because I know these things that I know this—my brother Donald and I were, authored, and designed with a Shared Purpose. I believe, that shared purpose is Truth, and Revelation: Exposing the hidden things. I believe exposing those hidden things was assigned to both the perpetrator of lies and the revealer of truth. *"For nothing is hidden that will not be made manifest, nor is anything secret that will not be known and come to life."* Luke 8:17.

That being said, though I don't have to like what my brother says or does to love him, I must take into account; what he says and what he does. If my brother's words and actions sin against the body of Christ, sin against our brothers and sisters, sin against the sons and daughters of our Father, God Jehovah, I am obligated to speak out against him.

"Open your mouth for the mute, for the rights of all who are destitute. Open your mouth, judge righteously, defend the rights of the poor and needy. Give justice to the weak and the fatherless; maintain the rights of the afflicted and the destitute. Learn to do good; seek justice, correct oppression. Like a muddied spring or a polluted well is a righteous man who gives way to the wicked." Proverbs 31:8–9

I am a member of the body of Christ. I am a child of God. I am my brothers' and sisters' keeper. I am therefore compelled to speak out against all injustice without regard. If I know the right thing to do but do nothing, I sin against my Lord; I sin against my brothers and sisters; I sin against the sons and daughters of God; I sin against God. Hence, at a time of God's choosing, I will be held accountable for having done nothing.

It is by God's decree for our own good that we are urged to pray for our leaders. No picking and choosing, no only praying for leaders we like or agree with. God's decrees are steadfast; they do not bend. They are His eternal, unchangeable, holy, wise, sovereign, purpose comprehending *all* things at once. What was, is, and is still to come in their causes, conditions, successions, relations, and determining their established future. What does that mean exactly? That means God knows everything. That means there's *nothing* God does not know. That means because God knows everything, because there's *nothing* He doesn't know, there are *no* contingencies to His decrees. We either obey God's decrees, written for our good, or we don't. The choice is ours, not God's.

When we pray for our leaders, we pray for ourselves; we can't pray for one without praying for the other. Likewise, when we pray against our leaders, we pray against ourselves; we can't pray against one without praying against the other. One thing God ISN'T is wishy-washy! He means what He says; He says what He means. There is no ambiguity in Him.

To reap the benefits of prayer, we must understand the nature prayer—that prayer is love; that it is kind, considerate, thoughtful, truthful, and righteous. For our prayers to be productive, the intent of our prayer must reflect the nature of prayer—love, kindness, consideration, thoughtfulness, truthfulness, and righteousness. Our prayers must be sincerely spoken. Sincere prayer is pleasing to God, brings us closer to Him, and sanctions Him to move on our behalf. Sincere prayer sows back into the sower. Sincere prayer reaps a bountiful harvest. Insincere prayer reaps multitudinous weeds.

I write this knowing some of us will see others of us only look; some of us will listen, others of us only hear; some of us will agree others of us will disagree; some of us will believe others of us will disbelieve. More importantly, I write this knowing our differing views, opinions, and beliefs are good things; if they weren't, God wouldn't have designed us human. He would have designed us opinionless robots, neither liking nor disliking, neither believing nor disbelieving, without want, need, or aspiration; without spirit, soul, or body created to worship Him for all eternity, without feeling, knowing or caring why. But God didn't do that. Why? Because there's no beauty in sameness, no uniqueness, no peculiarity, no emotion, no love.

God designed us, spirit, soul, and body, each soul having its own mind, thoughts, views, and opinions. Externally sculpted to perfection, made visually appealing, wrapped in colorful skin, no two shades, exactly, the same. Yet, internally, God designed us identical, a montage of life-sustaining functions, visually unappealing, dull-colored, invaluable shapes and sizes. God placed what makes us most precious beneath our skin out of eyesight, away from human thoughts, views, and opinions. Each life-sustaining function, functioning exactly the same inside every man, woman, and child of every race, ethnicity, and nationality. Yet we humans place our value in what we can see rather than what we can't.

Why would God do such a thing? Why would He scalp us externally different with beautiful faces and shapely bodies? Why would He adorn us with contrasting skin, hair, and eye colors? Why would He publicly display the most alluring, least important, least valuable parts of us? External decorations that satisfy the eyes and entertain the flesh, yet play no part in keeping us alive—physically or spiritually. Why would He go to such lengths to hide our identical, unchanging, unappealing, misshapen, dull-colored, life-sustaining, internal uniformity—the most important, most valuable, most unique, most precious parts of us? Internal life-sustaining functions that, when needed, can be transplanted and/or transfused from one human into another human and continue to function impervious to gender, race, ethnicity, or nationality. Why indeed? Ever given thought as to why the Holy Spirit resides within, rather than without? The person God authored and designed us to be, resides within. What makes us amazing resides within. What makes us priceless resides within. What makes us precious resides within. What makes us unique resides within. What brings us closer to and allows us to communicate with God resides within. God is love. God is beauty. God is truth. God is grace. God is mercy. God is no respecter of persons. God's love, beauty, truth, grace, mercy, and impartiality can't be seen through, eyes of flesh. Ergo to see as God sees though we look through eyes of flesh; let us see through eyes of love. Henceforth, when we look at one another let us see what God sees—we are beautiful. *"Blessed are the pure in heart, for they shall see God."* Matthew 5:8.

God designed us transplantable and transfusable that we might be of service to one another in both life and death. Our internal organs, bodily fluids, and essential substances work together, in perfect harmony, for the good of the *"whole"* body. There's no inward fighting, no bickering, no complaining, no name-calling, no bias; no division. There is no better or worse internal function. There is no higher or lower internal function. When internal organs are transplanted, or bodily fluids transfused from one human to another, there is no change in functionality; there is only the good of the body. The heart of an African American female transplanted into the pericardial cavity of a Caucasian American male will function exactly the same, though race and gender appear contrary.

We are more like our Father than not, more love than hate, more good than the bad, more forgiving than vengeful, more empathetic than apathetic. We are His handiwork. Spiritual beings purposely and purposefully designed from the inside out wrapped in colorful skin, each color equally beautiful, each person beneath the skin equally loved. We've become so consumed by our social outer differences we rarely consider our life-sustaining inner-sameness. What makes us invaluable resides internally amid our orderly sameness, not externally amid our disorderly differences.

We are spiritual beings residing in bodies of flesh; created by God—in the beginning, pure spirit, pure soul; pure body. Male and female, made in God's image, according to His likeness. Our spirit having direct contact with our Creator. Our soul, appointed, intellect, emotion, temperament, understanding, memory, perception, reasoning; how we think, etc. Our body designed to live forever, shelter for our spirit and soul. We were given free will, power, authority, and dominion over the earth. Only one thing was forbidden. Do not eat from the Tree of Knowledge of good and evil because on that day, we would surely die. I imagine some of us are thinking. We!—we didn't eat the fruit! Adam and Eve ate the fruit! Well, brothers and sisters, I say, we, because the first man and woman birthed "all" of humankind. We're their offspring, every man, woman, and child; every race/color; ethnicity and nationality—one big [happy?] family. Unfortunately, to our detriment, we continue to walk, in the same willful disobedient footsteps, of our in the beginning; long-dead parents. To make matters worse, we've been passing that centuries-old, willful disobedience down to our children for generations. How, pray tell have we done that?…

"The Lord is slow to anger and abounding in loving devotion, forgiving iniquity and transgression. Yet will by no means leave the guilty unpunished, He will visit the iniquity of the fathers upon their children to the third and fourth generation." Numbers 14:18

In my humble opinion…

Though the first man and woman started the *"willful disobedience"* ball rolling; we this present generation, and the preceding generation—are the ones who keep it rolling.

We all know about the fall of Adam and Eve. But I wonder, *How many of us have considered the enormity of their actions?*

Adam and Eve did far more than eat, forbidden fruit. They broke the first law of God—obedience. The first law of heaven, the foundation upon which righteousness and progression rest. They also broke the divine law of God—the infinite and eternal law. When they broke the first law of God, they fell from their state of innocent obedience into a state of guilty disobedience. One bite was all it took for Satan to slither his way into their lives. One bite was all it took for Adam and Eve's pure bodies to become corrupt and turn to flesh. One bite was all it took for Satan—*evil personified*—to seduce Adam and Eve's flesh. One bite gave Satan direct contact with Adam and

Eve's flesh. As for Adam and Eve dying, not just yet. Remember, God said, "*Surely* not immediately."

The moment Adam and Eve bit into the forbidden fruit, they began to die. This was no ordinary piece of fruit, and their's would be no ordinary death. The fruit was a slow-acting poison; their actual death was a long way off. The Bible doesn't say how old Eve was when she died but lists Adam's age of death as 930 years. Imagine living that long and not a day passes that you don't remember what you did and the life you gave up. Once Satan laid hold of Adam and Eve's flesh, all hell broke loss—literally! But Satan didn't stop with Adam and Eve; he wanted their firstborn and secondborn son, Cain and Abel; and because of the sins of the parents, he got them. Cain committed the first murder when he killed his brother, Abel.

Why did Cain kill Abel? His flesh. Satan told him to! In a fit of rage and jealousy, Cain rose up against Abel, hit him in the head with a rock, and killed him! Consequently, Cain was banished from the presence of the Lord, forced to leave his parents, and sent to dwell in the land of Nod—the dwelling place of vagabonds and fugitives. Yet, even though Cain murdered his brother, God was merciful, placing a mark of protection upon him that no one should kill him. One bite was all it took to inject physical death into Adam and Eve's pure, eternal bodies. I cannot help but ponder what forbidden things we might be saying or doing that bring harm and/or, in some cases, death to ourselves and others because of race, gender, religious belief, personal preference, political affiliations, and the all-powerful outside appearance! Even though we continue to follow in the footsteps of Adam and Eve, God remains merciful.

"The works of the flesh are evident: sexual immorality, impurity, sensuality, idolatry, sorcery, enmity, strife, jealousy, fits of anger, rivalries, dissensions, divisions, envy, drunkenness, orgies and things like these." Galatians 5: 19-26

Paul said, "I know that nothing good lives in me, that is, in my flesh; for I have the desire to do what is good, but I cannot carry it out. For I do not do the good I want to do. Instead, I keep on doing the evil I do not want to do. And if I do what I do not want, it is no longer I who do it, but the sin living in me that does it." Romans 7:18-19-20

Our bodies were created pure, eternal vessels. No longer pure, our death is imminent. Our flesh has one all-consuming purpose—consume its occupant! Its methods of consumption, our self-destruction, hasn't changed since that day in the Garden of Eden. It uses the same self-destructive methods against us as it did Adam and Eve—self-destructive methods it learned from *evil personified*. When Eve took that first bite of forbidden fruit and Adam followed suit gives a whole new meaning to "if it ain't broke, don't fit it." No reason for evil to change its ways when, generation after generation, we remain the same.

Every generation since the fall of Adam and Eve has fallen. Every generation since the fall of Adam and Eve has broken the first law and the divine law of God. When will it end? Where will it end? Which generation will finally stand up and say, "Enough!" God didn't design us to be our parents. He didn't design us to think like our parents. He didn't design us to mimic our parents. He didn't design us to have the same likes and dislikes of our parents. He didn't design us to follow in our parents' footsteps. God designed us unique. He designed us to think for ourselves. He designed us to decide for ourselves, designed us to decide what we like and/or dislike. He designed us to forge our own path, knowing whatever path we chose would lead us straight back to him. God gave us free will—the freedom to choose.

So, why pray tell, do we continue making the same bad choices generation after generation? Of what "good" use is free will when our primary choices appear to be more, oftentimes than not, based on worldly approval and self-gratification? Our seemingly insatiable need to be someone, anyone, other than the person God designed is mind-boggling—this supermodel, that politician, this businessman/woman, that rich man/woman, this movie star, that broadway star, this professional athlete, that professional singer; this television personality. We crave societal approval, recognition, and acceptance; worldly titles, money, and material things. Yet, what we crave isn't who we are. We're not a color/race, ethnicity, or nationality. We're not, a gender, or personal preference. We're not a religious belief, disbelief, or political affiliation. We're not worldly titles; how much money we have; don't have or material things. We are the sons and daughters of God! He justifies, approves, recognizes, and accepts us; as we are; where we stand; every second of every day! Begging the question: Why do we crave the sorrowful riches of the world, when the blessings of God, hold no sorrow? *"The blessings of the Lord enriches He adds no sorrow to it."* Proverbs 10:22 Why do we strive to be the world's less more so than God's more? What kind of sense does that make, considering? God owns everything! What does God owning everything mean? It means nothing in the world belongs to the world. It means this world has nothing legitimate to offer. It means God can give us everything the world illegitimately promises, but the world can't give us anything God lawfully promises.

We deserve better than our past; our children deserve better than our past; our children's children deserve better than our past; the generations yet to come deserve better than our past. And we, most assuredly, deserve better than this jacked-up world illegitimately has to offer. The world keeps pointing us toward one another, keeps encouraging us to blame, disrespect, hate, and kill. Satan has tricked us into believing we're fighting against flesh and blood/physical people. But Ephesians 6:12 tells us that we fight not against flesh-and-blood, but against the rulers, against the authorities, against the cosmic powers over this present darkness, against spiritual forces of evil in the heavenly places. This *present darkness*, brothers and sisters; is so intent on destroying us, it remains ever-present, generation after generation. Not because it hates us, but because God loves us. The world is a chessboard; we're pawns, rooks, knights, and bishops. The closest thing we have to a queen is Wisdom and the Virgin Mary. God is king. **Question:** What is the final move of chess? Before we can understand the final move of chess, we must first understand the goal of chess. The goal of chess is to checkmate the opponent's king. Checkmate occurs when the opponent's king is attacked from all sides. Checkmate! No escape! The king is defeated. We're in a battle for our souls' brothers and sisters!—a battle Christ already won! How's that even possible? Why, are we fighting a battle already won? Evil knows God can't be dethroned yet the battle rages on. Could it be we're still fighting because the battle rages on!—within us? Could it be even amid our materialistic, often perverse, societally-driven-state-of-mind, we know—we're NOT alone! Could it be the most sacred part of us knows, God has not forsaken us, that He desires *"none"* of us should perish, that He is *"determined"* to save as many of us as He can; for as long as He can—till heaven and earth pass away. Could it be we continue to fight because the *"Whole"* of who we are, constantly reassures the individuality of who we are—Whose we are?! Could it be, through the battle rages on; we know—the war is already won? Could it be...

"And ye shall hear of wars and rumors of wars; see that ye be not troubled: for all these things must come to pass, but the end is not yet." Matthew 24:6

This age-old-ever-present-evil knows he's defeated, but he keeps fighting. Why is evil so intent on fighting an already lost war? Two words, Unconditional Love. Evil fights because he's taken into "accounting" what many of us *"caught up"* in the battle take for granted; the unconditional love God has for humankind. Evil has taken into accounting—God can be hurt; God weeps; God grieves. How does evil know these things? He knows because he was the first to hurt God; He was the first to grieve God. He knows because he introduced hurt and grief to the heavens. He knows because God wept for him and the fallen third of the heavenly host. Ergo, he knows, God weeps, hurts, and grieves for us.

God spoke of His grievance to the Prophets Jeremiah, Hosea, and Isaiah. Yet, at no time did His love for humanity wavier...

"Therefore, thou shalt say this word unto them; Let mine eyes run down with tears night and day and let them not cease for the virgin daughter of my people is broken with a great breach, with a very grievous blow." Jeremiah 14:17

"Truly, Ephraim is a dear son to me, a child that is dandled! Whenever I have turned against him, my thoughts would dwell on him still. That is why my heart yearns for him; I will receive him back with love; declares the Lord." Jeremiah 31: 20-21

"Call for the mourning women. And let them take up wailing for us, that our eyes may run down with tears, and our eyelids gush out with water." Jeremiah 9: 17-18

"The more I called them, the more they went from me; they kept sacrificing to the Baals and offering incense to idols. Yet it was I who taught Ephraim to walk, I took them up in my arms, but they did not know that I healed them. I led them with cords of human kindness, with bands of love. I was to them like those who lift infants to their cheeks. I bend down to them and fed them. Hosea 11:2-4

"In all their affliction he was afflicted, and the angel of his presence saved them; in his love and his pity he redeemed them; he lifted them up and carried them all the days of old." Isaiah 63:9

God has been fighting, hurting, weeping, and grieving for us for centuries. This "already won" generational battle was never about winning. Evil realizes what many of us "caught-up" in life have yet to comprehend—that his end is close-at-hand. Soon there will be nowhere left for him to turn; no one left for him to corrupt.

Question: What do desperate people do when their back is up against the wall?

Answer: They go for broke; throw caution to the wind; do as much damage as they can; in whatever time they have left.

Evil's back is up against the wall, he's going for broke; throwing caution to the wind. He's determined to cause as much division, devastation, and death as he can in whatever time he has left. He will not let up! He will not give up! He will fight until there's no fight left in him!—until he thinks there's no fight left in us! He has one last move. Hazard a guess as to who/what that move is?

Hint: His last move is the same as his first. *Lies!*

Satan is the father of lies, *"But the serpent said to the woman, "You will not surely die."* Genesis 3:4.

God is the Father of truth, *"For truly, I say to you, until heaven and earth pass away, not an iota, not a dot, will pass from the Law until all is accomplished."* Matthew 5:18.

God stands with us until the end—until our time on earth has run its course. Only then will He release those of us who chose evil over good. Yet even then; when we no longer feel His Presence; He will be with us. We will remember Him; He will remember us!—even unto eternal death. Why? Because He promised, *"I will never leave thee, nor forsake thee"* Hebrews 13:5

I assure you, brothers and sisters, regardless of the bad choices we've made; regardless of the hurt, pain, and devastation we've caused; regardless of what we've done to others; regardless of what others have done to ourselves; regardless of how big and bad Satan *thinks* he is; regardless of how much Satan *thinks* he's taken from us; regardless of how many of us Satan *thinks* he's taken from God, the Blood of Christ covered it all—every human imperfection. God's grace and mercy blankets the *human condition*. Satan doesn't decide where we spend eternity—we do! We can be remade; we can be restored, if we so choose. That being said, we cannot serve two masters. We must choose. I pray we choose correctly.

The flesh has one mandate: destroy its occupant! Me dedicating my life to Christ didn't change my flesh one iota! It didn't run; it didn't hide; it didn't surrender. The flesh *cannot* change. The flesh *cannot* improve. The flesh *cannot* make our life better. The flesh *cannot/will not* vacate the premises! No way! No how! Our flesh will *never* change! But Yes! We can! We can change the way and how we speak to one another. We can change the way and how we treat one another. We can change the way and how we view one another! We can change the way and how we refer to one another! We can change the way and how we think toward one another. We can love one another as we want to be loved, unconditionally without regard! We can forgive one another as we want to be forgiven, unconditionally without regard! We can accept one another as we want to be accepted, unconditionally without regard! Come hell or high water! We can defend and protect one another as we want to be defended and protected, unconditionally without regard!

Will our flesh back down? Nope! Will it pull out all the stops to discredit and destroy? Most definitely! Will there still be moments of weakness? Most assuredly! Will there still be moments of doubt, fear, and anger? Without a doubt! Will there still be trials and tribulations? Count on it! The flesh cannot change; God doesn't expect flesh to change. He expects us to change by way of His Ransomed Son, and indwelling of the Holy Spirit, abounding grace and tender mercies. There will come a day!—when the heavens open! On that day! Christ Jesus will return to the earth to rid us of our corrupt flesh! On that day! Lord God Almighty!—will resurrect and transform our fallen bodies! But until that day arrives the flesh remains unchanged; it is the host; the out-dwelling of sin; it cannot change. Praise God!— We are NOT our flesh! We can change. We can do better! We can be better! How? Free will; the choices we make. Though evil constantly deceives us—it can't choose for us. We choose for ourselves! Not to mention, we've got some Serious Spiritual Backup! Wherein evil resides externally amidst the flesh. Thusly, the Holy Spirit resides internally amidst the spirit! Guess what the word thusly symbolizes. No need to guess. Here ya go…

The definition of thusly: Until you move you will appear thusly in your location.

What does that mean for us? It means the Holy Spirit is anchored within us. It means He will not remove Himself from us until His time on earth has run its course.

Thusly also symbolizes the North Star, the center of the starfield. The North Star doesn't move like other stars; it essentially displays no movement. The North Star is located nearly at the north celestial pole; the entire northern sky rotates around it; True North is directly beneath it. During slavery it served as a beacon of hope, guiding runaway slaves' true north to freedom; it *"always"* points toward home; a constant reminder—*home is never far away.* It is the brightest star nearest the North *"Celestial"* Pole; the universe beyond earth's atmosphere; the visible heaven; the sky, sun, moon, and stars. Point to ponder…everything God created, He created with us in mind; to comfort, protect, and guide. On earth as in the heavens—all roads lead back to God. All roads lead home.

The spirit does not abide the flesh, neither does the flesh abide the spirit. The spirit is strong, willing, and able; the flesh is weak, willful, and wanting. The spirit unites and integrates; the flesh divides and separates. The spirit looks and sees; the flesh looks yet rarely sees. The spirit hears and listens; the flesh hears yet rarely listens. The spirit desires the approval of God; the flesh seeks the approval of man. My brother, Donald, and I travel two different paths, yet both paths lead back to our Father, God Jehovah. When our time on earth ends, our Father will be waiting. We will be held accountable for every spoken word and deed. The lies, trappings, and temptations of this world will have crumbled into dust. There will be no one to speak on our behalf, other than ourselves. We will be stripped bare. No titles. No higher or lower. No richer, or poorer. No male or female. No black or white. No reprieves, only accountability, culpability, the final judgment and sentencing. But that's not the scariest part. The scariest thing about our final judgment and sentencing—it won't be determined by God. It will be determined by us. God doesn't decide where we spend eternity—we do. Our eternity in death; as our life on earth—will be a matter of choice. We decide our fate—not God, and most assuredly, not Satan.

As surely as I know the aforementioned, I know this: God didn't create hell; evil created hell. Our indifference, hatred, greed, prejudice, and various other facets of sin we justify, disregard, accept, and practice; generation after generation sustains hell's exponential growth.

Luke 16: 23-31, tells of a rich man who went to hell and a beggar who went to heaven,

> "There was a rich man who was dressed in purple and fine linen and lived in luxury every day. At his gate was laid a beggar named Lazarus, covered with sores and longing to eat what fell from the rich man's table. Even the dogs came and

licked his sores. The time came when the beggar died, and the angels carried him to Abraham's side. The rich man also died and was buried. In Hades, where he was in torment, he looked up and saw Abraham far away, with Lazarus by his side. So, he called to him, 'Father Abraham, have pity on me and send Lazarus to dip the tip of his finger in water and cool my tongue because I am in agony in this fire. But Abraham replied, 'Son, remember that in your lifetime you received your good things, while Lazarus received bad things, but now he is comforted here, and you are in agony. And besides all this, between us and you a great chasm has been set in place so that those who want to go from here to you cannot, nor can anyone cross over from there to us. He answered, 'Then I beg you, father, send Lazarus to my family, for I have five brothers. Let him warn them so that they will not also come to this place of torment. Abraham replied, 'They have Moses and the Prophets; let them listen to them. "No, father Abraham,' he said, 'but if someone from the dead goes to them, they will repent. "He said to him, 'If they do not listen to Moses and the Prophets, they will not be convinced even if someone rises from the dead.'"

When I read the story of the rich man and the beggar, it gave me; serious pause. Serious pause, because I didn't hear any fear in his voice. I heard acceptance, sorrow, regret, and concern. Acceptance, that he put himself in hell. Sorrow, that he chose the world over God. Regret, that he lived an unrepentant life. Concern; if his brothers weren't warned they would also end up in hell. I believe the torment and fire he spoke of wasn't physical, but spiritual. Physical death would be far kinder. Physical death doesn't require thought;

it only requires you to feel the pain. Spiritual Death requires you to think, feel, remember and ponder. Burning remembrances, blistering emotions, scorching thoughts; searing ponderances'. Forever knowing, forever feeling, forever pondering; eternal flames!—there is no escape. There is no absolution. Things done can't be undone. Things said can't be unsaid. The time for repentance has passed.

Free will, our freedom to choose, provides us endless possibilities. But it's our present-day choices that impact, not only our present-day lives, but the lives of future generations still to come. We can't stop the future, but we can prevent bad future outcomes by making good present-day choices. Nothing will truly change until we truly change.

The Nature and Character of Wall Builders

The first time I saw Mr. Trump, I saw my past come full circle into my present. I saw the corrupt personification of the seven wall builders I survived from childhood into adulthood. I saw a clear and present danger. Eight different men from eight different walks of life, a United States president, a pimp, two child molesters, two assembly-line workers, a truck driver, and a businessman; what could these eight men possibly have in common? One word, *character*. Eight outwardly different men characteristically the same. Salesmen, dividers, separatists, liars, manipulators, intimidators, instigators, fearmongers, rapists, and abusers. How these eight men became the men they became, only God knows. Various life conditions, circumstances, and situations I would imagine.

I say that because our nature is what we're born with; whereas our character is what we develop over time through our life experiences, the good and bad; what we learn from those experiences, and how we choose to use what we learn. Our character doesn't succumb to our nature; our nature succumbs to our character. There is no way of knowing what transpired between the nature these men were born with and the character they developed. But what I'm certain of is this: at some juncture of these eight men's lives, they made a conscious choice to choose, the character of men, they became. They chose the character of immorality. They chose to become rapists and abusers of the mind, body, spirit, soul, and environment.

The immoral character these eight men chose is the moral evil that raped, pillaged, and terrorized me throughout my childhood and a large portion of my adult life. That same moral evil, now bigger, badder, meaner, and hungrier is currently raping, pillaging, and terrorizing this country. I see past its elaborate disguises; I listen beyond its loud misleading clamoring, lies disguised as truth, apathy disguised as concern, wrong disguised as right, ugliness disguised as beauty; prejudice disguised as justice. I was just a girl when evil barged into my life. I'm much older now; time has taken its toll. My body moves a bit slower these days; often aching in places I never knew existed, my skin sags, my youthful appearance; long gone, and yet amid these physical debilitations; my spirit thrives and springs eternal.

When some of us hear the words *rape* and *abuse*, we immediately think person; rarely do we think place or thing, emotions, families, neighborhoods, churches, schools, cities, states, nations, or the environment. But the truth of the matter is everyone/everything can be raped and/or abused. Wall builders target our emotions, tantalizing our likes, wants and desires, heightening our dislikes, fears, and insecurities, intensifying our aggravations and agitations; continually hindering and distracting us. Some wall builders are satisfied with one target; others require multiple targets to achieve satisfaction. Regardless of the intended target, be it a person, place, or thing, all wall builders abide the same strategy: divide, separate, and conquer! Disgrace, devalue, and discredit the intended target. Generate an atmosphere of suspicion and mistrust. Promote chaos, advocate division, encourage separation. Isolate the intended target from everyone and everything beneficial. Build an unscalable, impenetrable; inescapable wall. Cordon off every source of help and hope. Confiscate the selected target's power and authority by any means necessary. Once power and authority are secured mold target into someone/something of their making and choosing.

My dad was my first wall builder. He designed the blueprint, devised the strategy future wall builders would expand on. His blueprint shaped the majority of my childhood and most of my adult life. Birth fathers are supposed to be examples for their daughters, teach them about honor and respect, what it means to be loved and cherished. My dad didn't do that. I didn't know anything about anything; I didn't know who I was or why I was. When you don't know anything, when you don't know your who or your why, you don't know what to change; you don't know how to change; you don't know when to change; you don't know why to change. I grew from a scared little girl into a paranoid woman. I was convinced the men I allowed into my life somehow knew one another; that they had taken detailed notes about me and secretly passed those notes to one another. It's the only thing that made sense. How else could they all know so much about me, mere days after meeting me; they had to know one another. Forty-four years of my life with the same/different man using the exact same strategy; why couldn't I see that? It took years of mental and physical abuse for me to finally see the character of my wall builders; see that they weren't many—they were one. That their statistical tactics were the same because they were the same. The wall builders weren't going to change. It was up to me to change; up to me to live or die. I made a mental list of the wall builders' tactical strategies, took a mental snapshot, and promised myself I'd never be blindsided again. I was wrong.

The Unchanging Strategy of Wall Builders

First tactical strategy. Bribe and recruit people I trusted who secretly only care about themselves.

Second tactical strategy. Enlist individuals easily manipulated—the desperate, fearful, poor, needy, and discontented. Hard-working, angry men and women, denied the simplest creature comforts, who will, under the right conditions; look the other way.

Third tactical strategy. Engage and entice those who consider themselves good, decent, and God-fearing yet currently find themselves wanting. Practices they once considered bias and unfair; they find themselves reexamining; due to financial hardship.

Final and deadliest tactical strategy. Pathogens. Bacterial agents, individuals willing to spread lies and propaganda. Do whatever the wall builder says to enforce his agenda, and ensure his success.

Conscienceless, greedy, selfish, prideful, apathetic, heartless individuals who only care about themselves and pleasing the wall builder.

The three wall builders who destroyed my childhood convinced me early on I was less than, and I believed them. Why wouldn't I? I was a child and therefore thought, and reasoned, as a child. There was no one around to tell me the wall builders were lying. No one to tell me what they were doing wasn't my fault. No one to comfort me, no one to teach me, no one to show me the way I should go. Lacking knowledge, and understanding I take my less-than-childhood-mentality into adulthood. I grow physically as an adult, but mentally I'm still a child, and therefore continue to reason as a child.

When I was a child, no one protected me; no one came to my defense. When I was a girl, no one cared; no one noticed. When I became a woman, I didn't know how to protect, defend, care for, or notice myself. When I was a child, everybody stood around waiting for someone else to do something. Stood around waiting for someone else to say something. Stood around waiting for someone else to take a stand. When I was a girl, everyone stood around waiting for someone else to do something. Stood around waiting for someone else to say something. Stood around waiting for someone to take a stand. When I became a woman, I stood around waiting for someone else to do something. Stood around waiting for someone else to say something. Stood around waiting for someone else to take a stand.

When I was a child, no one considered the someone else they were standing around waiting for might be them. When I was a girl, no one considered the someone else they were standing, around waiting for might be them. When I became a woman, I didn't consider the someone else I was standing around waiting for might be me.

When I was a child, I did not know how to think for myself. The wall builders did my thinking for me. Wall builders gave familiar men and women permission not to do anything, permission not to say anything, permission not to take a stand, permission not to help me; permission to leave me where I was. When I was a girl I was afraid to think for myself. If the wall builder thought I was thinking for myself, trying to figure a way out, he beat me mercilessly or tied me to a chair, put me in the closet and left me there until just before mom got home. To this day, I still don't understand how he was able to beat me without ever leaving a mark. It seemed to me, no matter how many blankets and towels he wrapped me in; there should have been evidence of his beatings. When I became a woman I gave myself permission not to do anything, permission not to say anything, permission not to take a stand, permission not to help myself, permission not to care about myself, permission not to consider my needs, permission to leave me where I was, permission not to think for myself; permission to let men do my thinking for me.

I see that same standing around waiting from someone else to do something mentality spreading across America today. A few of us are starting to realize the someone we're standing around waiting for is us, yet—as we ponder the wait—evil marches on. Time is fleeting, yet we continue to wait for someone else to do what we should be doing ourselves. As time waits for no man, neither does evil. The same deadly weeds that strangled the life out of my childhood are strangling the life out of America; on a more deadly, global-encompassing, consequential scale. Blatant lies, half-truths, indifference, and human disregard are trampling our rights, liberties, and freedoms. Rights, liberties, and freedoms, countless Americans—foreign and domestic, multihued, male and female, free and slave; sacrificed, suffered, fought, and died for.

I see the same malignant weeds of fear, anger, unrest, mistrust, and greed that muffled my voice, strangled my soul, chained and bound my spirit, hoping to kill off what little hope and compassion I had left, dividing and separating our homes, neighborhood, schools, churches, and cities under the guise of protected exclusivity/border walls hoping to muffle the voices, strangle the souls, chain and bound the spirits of America's citizens, residents, and visitors who remember and openly declare! Inclusion and open arms are what made America great!

When it comes to the world evil has numerous goals. When it comes to America he has only one. Total annihilation! Everyone and everything she stands for! We, the people! Freedom! Justice! Liberty!

Life and the Pursuit of Happiness! In God we trust! Evil's unwavering mandate—leave no one; leave nothing standing! Destroy the American Nation!—the remaining nations will follow. This isn't evil's first go-around-never-say-never attempt at destroying America—America is the proverbial thorn in evil's side. Though every battle waged against her ends in defeat, evil keeps-on-keeping on. Why? Two words: Righteous Majority. Evil keeps trying to [deceive] us into believing we are more unrighteous than righteous; that when it comes to self-preservation; in some instances—doing wrong is right.

We the righteous majority!—are, the truth, evil so desperately tries to keep hidden. The truth that we are loved above and beyond!—our sin. That God is going to do everything He can [without interfering with our free will] to save us! Truth: Evil is NOTHING without us! Truth: Evil can't complete its goal of human annihilation without us! Truth: The only power and authority evil has is the power and authority; we give him.

"You will know the truth, and the truth will set you free." John 8:32

The paradox of evil—though we are born with a sin-nature, though we are prone to do wicked things, God continues to love us, continues to forgive us, continues to empower us, continues to protect us, continues to show us grace and mercy. Grace and mercy that *renew each morning—that no weapon formed against us shall prosper. "No weapon formed against you shall prosper, and every tongue which rises against you in judgment you shall condemn. This is the heritage of the servants of the Lord and their righteousness is from Me. Thus says the Lord."* Isiah 54:17

To succeed (which he never will) evil needs more than our sin-nature; he needs our character formation; characteristics developed over time; learned-behaviors. But not just any characteristics and learned behaviors. Evil needs the broken things, the hateful things, the hurtful things, the disappointing things, the unforgiving things, the selfish things, the apathetic things, the greedy things, the lacking things, the adulterous things, the lying boastful things, the immoral things, the shattered things; things that can be further deceived, manipulated, and molded into worse things. Evil needs a particular type of individual; with a particular mindset to sow his weeds of hate and corruption. He needs angry, sad, fearful, fed-up individuals looking for someone; anyone to blame for his/her problems. Satan needs an indifferent-hate-rich-environment for his weeds to thrive and spread. But, evil has limited mobility; it has no physical voice to speak on its behalf; no limbs to move about. We are evil's voice. We are evil's limbs. We are evil's only means of spreading.

What I couldn't see as a child, couldn't comprehend as a girl, misunderstood as a teen, couldn't recognize as a teenage wife and mother, and disregarded as a divorced woman I now see, and understand, in these my latter years. I see President Trump, my commander in chief for who and what he is; not who and what I want him to be. I listen to his words. I hear what he says, not what he pretends to say. I look to see whom he serves; at no time did I see we the people. What I saw was a man voted into the highest office in the land by the American people; entrusted with the power and authority to speak on behalf of the American nation. Power and authority misused, abused, and falsely acquired on January 20, 2017, when Mr. Trump—with bias, malice, and forethought—fraudulently spoke the presidential oath of office.

"I do solemnly swear (or affirm) that I will faithfully execute the Office of President of the United States and will to the best of my ability, preserve, protect, and defend the Constitution of the United States."

For three years I watched President Trump, the commander and chief of the United States make a mockery of the oath he swore to preserve and protect. Disrespecting not only the United States Presidency, not only the American people but all people and all nations. I watched my Commander and Chief give evil a Presidential Pardon, his Seal of Approval to run amuck, spread hate, lies, and chaos, permission to kill and maim; without fear of consequence.

When I was a girl I was naive. When I was a girl I was one; I stood alone. I am now a woman both knowledgeable and wise. No longer naive. No longer alone! No longer one! I am many. I stand with my brothers and sisters, the sons and daughters of God. Every race!

Every ethnicity! Every nation! We are the United States of America! We are a nation of millions favored by God to rescue trillions. As a united people, not only will we save our nation; we are destined to save many nations!

We are the nation God favored above all nations. The nation He stationed atop a high hill for all the world to see. The nation He rose from the ashes. The nation He ordained a source of help and hope. The nation He ordained a place of quiet rest. The nation He ordained a fountain of comfort. The nation He ordained a residency of well-being. The nation He ordained empathic receiver. The nation He ordained guardian and protector. The nation He ordained a light amid the darkness. We are chosen for such a time as this. Chosen to stand united! United in freedom, liberty, justice, and equality for all mankind!

> For though I am free from all men, yet have
> I made myself servant unto all, that I might gain
> the more. (1 Corinthians 9:19)

From a past of covertness, thievery, slavery, and death, America gained more—by way of God's favor! Let us not be defined, weighted, or measured by worldly standards. Let us not become weary in doing good, lest we forget; God's grace and mercy are given; God's favor is approved. We must remain diligent in our humanness. We must continually strive to show ourselves approved.

This is my testimony, my sad accounting of eight wall builders: my biological father, the stepfather, the trusted neighbor/truck driver, my ex-husband, two assembly-line workers, a businessman, and an American president. My biological father and the stepfather are both dead. I don't know what became of the trusted neighbor. My ex-husband remarried, is alive and well. Last I heard, the businessman is in a nursing home, dying from cancer—one of the factory workers became a widower a few years back, and the other is said to be happily married. I addressed my ex-husband and the trusted neighbor early on. I will now address my biological father, the stepfather, and President Trump. I will not be addressing the two married assembly line workers.

The Beginning, Not the End

My biological father was the beginning and end of my childhood; my fall from light-filled innocence into the empty darkness of guilt, fear, and shame. He was my first wall builder. He was the first to lessen me, the first to hurt me, the first to wreck me, the first to abandon me. He was the prelude, the ushering in of the stepfather, the trusted neighbor, ex-husband, and all the wall builders that followed. He is the reason evil took closer notice of me, mid-November 1955. I'm six years old; today my life changes forever. Today my daddy pours the foundation upon which I will stand for the rest of my life. Today the clock starts ticking down the two remaining years of my childhood. Shortly after my eighth birthday, my childhood becomes something else. I become someone else. My innocence is replaced with something else.

I remember the day my life imploded like it was yesterday. Shortly after breakfast, Daddy drives Mom, my older sister, younger brother, and me to the Birmingham, Alabama, train station. Daddy seems unusually happy today, humming, whistling and tapping his fingers on the steering wheel. Mom, on the other hand, hasn't uttered a sound since she got in the car. My sister, brother, and I are seated in the backseat. We know something's wrong; we know well enough not to speak.

Daddy pulls into the train station, parks the car, jumps out, opens the trunk, and pulls out some suitcases. Where did those come from? I never saw those before. He walks to the train station platform, puts the suitcases down, hands Momma four train tickets to Detroit, Michigan, walks back to the car, gets in, and drives off. No, I love yous, no goodbye kisses, no goodbye hugs, no looking back. Momma looks so sad; I don't remember her ever looking so sad. I'm only six, but I know this ain't right. My momma stopped pretending that day, not because she wanted to but because she had to.

Leaving me to ponder, "Who was that mean man who looked like my daddy?"

It's nightfall when we board the train. Why did daddy bring us here so early? After momma gets us settled, she sits down, turns her face to the window, and stares out at the darkness. I see a tear roll down the side of her face. She flicks it away with her finger and places her hand over her wet cheek. She thinks no one's looking; she thinks one sees her crying, but I do, I see my momma crying. I never saw momma cry before; I heard her and Daddy arguing from time to time, but I never saw her cry. Has she cried before and I just didn't notice? Just like I didn't recognize Daddy, I don't recognize Momma. Was she ever happy? Was Daddy always mean? I feel something watching me, but I'm too scared to turn around to see what it is.

Why can't we just go back home? I don't like what I'm feeling. I hope I never feel this way again. Sadly I will—for many years to come. Evil staked his claim today. I'm too young to understand; too innocent to comprehend; my father has given evil power and author-ity over me. Though I was only six-years-old at the time; I think I somehow knew; my life would never be the same. Still, it will take me years to realize outer appearance and inner character are not the same, that how a person looks and sounds on the outside isn't nec-essarily who they are on the inside. It will take even longer for me to realize; people are rarely who they appear to be; that the true charac-ter of a person isn't what you can see, but what you can't.

I'll be pushing forty by the time I realize it doesn't matter how good or bad we think we are, or how good or bad others say we are. Why? Because we're both good and bad. We're capable of doing tre-mendous good, and we're capable of doing horrendous evil. In my midforties, I realized evil is a strategist. It has a plan of action; it has an endgame. I believe that endgame is exposure; to bring the bad things inside—outside. I believe a person's character, be it good or bad, wants to be known for who and what it is. I also believe despite what we do to hide or disguise what dwells within us, who we are beneath the skin will eventually make its way to the surface.

So what do we do when someone we believed and trusted reveals themselves to be malignant, egoistic, corrupt, and destructive? What do we do when convenient lies and false promises are exposed by ugly, painful, inconvenient truths—truths of hatred, prejudice, and greed? What do we do when we realize we made a horrible mistake, realize we placed immense power, authority, and the safety of millions into uncaring, unapologetic, indifferent hands? How do we respond? Do we admit our mistake and look for pragmatic solutions to correct our mistake? Or do we deny our mistake and look for defensible ways to justify it? Do we continue to defend the agents of convenient lies and false promises? Or will we stand steadfastly on the ugly, painful, inconvenient truth?

When I look at President Trump, I see an ugly, painful, inconvenient truth hiding behind a wall of convenient lies and false promises. I see the chaos, wantonness, hatred, greed, and prejudice of America's horrendous past bulldozing its way into the present. I see past evils anticipating their resurrection, hoping to finish what they started during the American Indian wars from 1622–1924. 313 years of injustice, lies, covetousness, and thievery. I see evil cheering the death the hopes and dreams still to come. I see us [still] standing around waiting for someone else to do something; someone else to say something; someone else to take a stand; someone else to rescue us—from the mess we made! I see evils both known and unknown orchestrating the death of our children, our children's children, and our children's, children's children for generations!

Evil has observed and studied us for generations; it knows many of us better than we know ourselves. It knows our likes dislikes, strengths, and weaknesses. It sees what many of us refuse to see— that our strength resides in our unity, that united we are invincible! Evil knows the division and separation of races, genders, political parties, and religious denominations are its best means of destroying the human race. Evil doesn't want to destroy some of us; he wants to destroy *all of us!* Evil never rests. It's always looking for new ways to divide and separate us from one another. It's constantly on the lookout for human vessels—humans willing to nurture it, help it grow, and spread, through human interaction. It needs human suffering, pain, and misery to survive.

Evil doesn't discriminate. It uses anyone and anything capable of being used—the Christian and the atheist, the just and the unjust, the faithful and unfaithful, the confused, misused, disappointed, grief stricken, fearful, educated, uneducated, lawmakers and lawbreakers. Heterosexual, transsexual, homosexual, bisexual, virgin, adulterer, and fornicator. Every man, woman, child; lower class, middle class, upper class, the rich and the destitute. Presidents, kings, and queens. Every race, ethnicity, and nationality. Evil is no respecter of person. No one is off-limits. Nothing is off-limits. No one is safe. Nothing is sacred.

The troubles facing America today isn't a matter of color; it's a matter of character. We've gotten so comfortable blaming our problems on race, we don't consider anything else. Why? Because it's easy, and we're lazy! Blaming skin color doesn't require actual thought, just point and shout whatever comes up in our discriminatory little minds. Problem is, our skin has no idea what's going on. It doesn't feel, think, or have an opinion, it doesn't know what it is let alone why it is. It has no concept of color. It doesn't feel love, hate, or animosity. It doesn't know prejudice, jealousy, or envy. It doesn't recognize pretty, ugly, short, tall, fat, skinny, man, woman, or child. It can't see, hear, or speak. It doesn't know happiness, sorrow, guilt, fear, or shame. It has no understanding of right, wrong, good or evil. Skin is colorful wrapping, purposed to cover and protect our internal organs, nothing more, nothing less. Skin is like the clothing we buy; colorful, beautiful, protective covering. The difference being we can remove our outer clothing; we cannot remove our outer skin. What does that mean? It means hating someone because of skin color makes about as much sense as hating someone because they're wearing pink; because we hate pink. It means skin color has no more, control over who's wearing it or the choices being made; any more than the clothes we wear. The character of the person who dwells beneath the skin is the one making the decisions. Skin, like clothing, is just along for the ride. It has no idea where it's going, why it's going, or what the person wearing it is going to do once they get there. Our skin doesn't even know what it is! How totally, messed up is that?

We cry black people this, white people that, Asian people this, Hispanic people that, Native Americans this, East Indian people that, and whatever color of people are left over this and that! We hate, demean, disrespect, demoralize, and ostracize one another because of our skin color! How crazy is that! Hating one another for something that doesn't even know it exists! Yet we "think" we're the most intelligent lifeform on the planet! Really? In all my years, I haven't once witnessed an animal, tree, flower, bird, fish, or bug race war! God entrusted the earth to us, and look at what we've done to it! Look at how we treat the very thing that sustains us. No animal, plant, tree, flower, fish, bird, or bug caused the earth's environmental problems. We did this! We are destroying the earth. We are destroying ourselves and, in so doing, our children. Who does that? Who destroys the very thing they need to live? The very thing their children and their children's children need to live. Oh! That would be us!

We base so many life choices on the views and opinions of others, on looking and hearing rather than seeing and listening. Why do we do that? We do it because it takes care to listen and see what is. It takes nothing to look and hear what isn't. Then there's the world, doing anything and everything it can to distract us from ourselves, constantly minimizing our similarities and magnifying our dissimilarities. Look, but don't see. Hear, but don't listen. Why? Three words: thought, time, and effort. The more thought, time, and effort we put into one another, the less thought, time, and effort we put into the world. Thought, time, and effort require us to care. Thought, time, and effort require us to give thoughtful pause to our words and actions before we speak and act. Thought, time, and effort require us to make the effort to do what's right—without regard! Thought, time, and effort—three considerations asking a moment of pause. Pause to reconsider. Pause to reexamine. Pause to redirect. Pause to breathe.

Somewhere along the way, we stopped being worth one another's thoughts, time, and effort. Somewhere along the way, we stopped being our brother/sister's keeper. Somewhere along the way, we stopped holding ourselves accountable. Somewhere along the way, it became easier to disbelieve than believe. Somewhere along the way, we became spiritually lazy and flesh overindulgent. Somewhere along the way, creature comforts became more important than human life. Somewhere along the way, fantasizing became more satisfying than reality. Somewhere along the way, it became easier to live by sight than faith. Somewhere along the way, we chose beautiful convenient lies over ugly inconvenient truths. Somewhere along the way, the individuality of us became more valuable than the whole of us. Somewhere along the way, we became so distracted by the world's outer ugliness; we lost sight of our inner beauty. Somewhere along the way, we stopped being God's warriors standing on the frontline and became the world's watchers standing on the sideline.

Why? What could have driven us to such dire straits? What indeed? Somewhere along the way, the world's lies became our truths. Somewhere along the way, the world's riches became our aspirations. Somewhere along the way, wrong became right and right became wrong. Somewhere along the way, good became bad and bad became good. Somewhere along the way, justice became injustice and injustice became justice. Somewhere along the way, empathy was discouraged and apathy was encouraged. Somewhere along the way, generosity was mocked and greed was applauded. Somewhere along the way, love was ridiculed and hate was appalled. Somewhere along the way, pleasing the created became more important than pleasing the Creator. *Somewhere along the way and never the twain shall meet, met.*

My Dad, the Wall, the Stepfather, My President

"Déjà vu."

The first time I heard Mr. Trump say he wanted to build a wall to keep Americans safe and undesirables out, I was sitting in my recliner in the living room drinking my morning cup of coffee. I pick up the TV remote and turn on the television. One of the local news stations is running footage from one of Mr. Trump's campaign rallies. I'm about to take my second sip of coffee, when the smirk on Mr. Trump's face causes me to pause. His eyes scan the crowd. He smiles, clenches his fist, raises his arms above his head, and shouts, "We're going to build a wall!"

The crowd erupts! Their loud, angry voices flood the room. "Build that wall! Build that wall!"

But it isn't the rowdy crowd that holds my attention; it's Mr. Trump, the disdain etched across his face and condescending tone of his voice as he praises Americans and berates Mexicans. Television news cameras pan the clamoring crowd, periodically zooming in on their enamored faces, their mouths screaming the name of the man they hope will be America's next commander and chief. The more Mr. Trump berates Mexico, the more excited the crowd becomes. The more excited the crowd becomes, the more scornful Mr. Trump becomes. The longer I watch, the sadder I become. I simply cannot wrap my mind around anyone, let alone someone campaigning to become the next president of the United States exhibiting such contempt for fellow human beings. Even more disturbing is seeing and hearing his contempt cheered and applauded.

I've been around long enough to see and hear a whole lot of good and a whole lot of bad in my personal life in society and the government. That being said, my personal life has improved tremendously over the years, whereas my views regarding government have substantially diminished. But my hope in us, my hope in we the people remained strong and unwavering. My hope in us kept my hope in government afloat, hope that our leaders would set aside their differences and become the leaders we the people deserve, hope that our leaders become the leaders they promised they'd be on the campaign trail.

My hope in us quieted my disbelief in the government. My disbelief America's leaders would one day put the welfare of the American people above their own, above their hidden political agendas, personal ambitions, social status, and monetary greed. But that day, sitting in my living room, seeing so many us cheering and applauding separatism, hatred, and racism, I'm forced to reexamine my hope in us as a people. Have I been wrong about us all these years? Have I been seeing who I want us to be rather than who we are?

I've seen and experienced a lot of bad over the years, enough to have lost count but not so much I couldn't work my way back. But that day in my living room, I saw something I never imagined happening in America; a United States presidential candidate disrespect and degrade an entire nation encouraged, admired, cheered, and celebrated. Forcing me to acknowledge, despite my belief and hope in us as a people, we the people still have a long way to go. Something in me resurfaced that day, something old and vengeful. People, memories, and emotions I "thought" long forgotten, dead and buried, emerged from the grave and slithered their way to the forefront of my mind regurgitating past hurts, pains, sufferings, and shame throughout my being.

I snatch the remote from the side table and point it at the television, but my fingers aren't working; I can't push the Off button. I try to look away, but my head won't turn; my eyes are glued to the TV screen. I want to cover my ears, but my arms are frozen to my side. I can't move. I try to suppress the guilt and shame traveling up my throat. The rancidness spills into my mouth, causing me to gag. Something about Mr. Trump and his angry brood feels horribly familiar. The more I watch, the sicker I feel. The more I listen, the more fearful I become.

Everything slows; it feels like I'm in a slow-moving motion picture. It's morning, but there's no sunlight coming through the patio blinds. The living room is completely dark. The only thing disrupting the darkness is the faint light of the television screen and it's cold; so cold. I'm freezing, I can't move, I can't breathe, I'm suffocating. I'm drowning! How's that even possible? I can't be suffocating and drowning at the same time. Something evil is coming; I can feel it, and I'm terrified. What is it? Why am I so afraid? I don't have to wait long for an answer. But it's not a what, it's a who.

The low voices and slow-moving images of Mr. Trump and his supporters fade away. There's a loud crackle. The television screen goes black. The living room goes from off-black to pitch-black. I'm blind. I can't see. I open my mouth and scream, but nothing comes out. It doesn't matter; there's no one around to hear me. Even if there were someone else here, would they even see what I'm seeing? The room slowly changes color; the outer perimeter remains pitch-black. The center of the living room just beyond where I'm seated turns gray.

A tall black shadow steps from the pitch-blackness, into the gray, and walks toward me. My heart leaps into my throat. I'm gonna be sick! It's the stepfather! But he's not alone. Grandma and the rest of his supporters—my childhood silent witnesses are with him. I try to close my eyes; they won't close. I try to lift myself from my recliner; fear and shame hold me down. A tiny dark gray shadow pushes its way through the large black shadows. I instinctively know it's a girl. She doesn't have a face, just two large chestnut-brown eyes surrounded by the whitest white I've ever seen. But she doesn't need a face for me to know who she is. She's me, the terrified eight-year-old girl I left cowering in the corner of my bedroom closet all those years ago.

The bone-chilling, soul-shaming, spirit-degrading voice of the stepfather slices through the darkness. My tiny shadow takes cover in a corner on the far side of the room; the only thing I can see is the whites of her eyes. I clench the arms of the recliner and push myself upward as hard as I can, but fear pushes me back down. I think to myself, I'm having some kinda messed up nightmare! But it's not a nightmare, and I'm not a confident sixty-eight-year-old-woman; I'm a terrified eight-year-old-little girl. My eyes dart from side to side, frantically looking for a way out. What's that smell? Lord! Help me! Please help me! It's Old Spice, the stepfather's scent, the scent that entered my bedroom night after night just before he walked in, the scent that lingered on my skin long after he was done with me, the scent I was forced to smell every night of my life for four years. The scent consumes me; it feels like I'm going to pass out. No such luck. That's when I hear them, the three hushed words that terrified four-years of my twelve-year childhood.

"Toni, Toni, baby."

My eyes fill with tears, and I wait, wait just as I did when I was a little girl. The stepfather stoops down in front of me, "I'm still here, Toni, baby! I'm still here! Nothin's changed! I say who ya are! I say what you are. You belong to me. You'll always belong to me. Nobody wanted to hear ya then, nobody wants to hear ya now! Look at you! You're old and fat! You were nobody then, you're NOBODY! Now! Nobody came to save you then! Nobody's comin' to save you now!"

I hear buzzing. I see light. Where's it coming from? It's the television, no images, no voices, just light and crackling sounds. My right hand twitches. I look down. I'm still holding the remote. I slide my thumb upward. I feel the Off button. I push down as hard as I can. Sunlight floods the room and I fall asleep. No rhyme or reason, I simply fall asleep. I don't know how long I slept. It didn't feel like more than a few minutes. I look down; the remote is still in my hand. I place it on the side table, lift the lever on my recliner, lower the footrest, bow my head and pray.

I can still feel the anger and hate from Mr. Trump and his supporters, but the face I see before me; is that of the stepfather. I hear old familiar sounds; fast-moving footsteps, creaking floorboards, squeaking door hinges, screeching bedsprings, and labored grunts. I smell old familiar aromas; Pall Mall cigarettes, body sweat, and Old Spice cologne. I feel the painful thrust and paralyzing fear of child-molestation. All the sounds, smells, and feelings that imprisoned my childhood, stunted my adult-growth, and continued to cripple and haunt me long after the stepfather was dead and buried; enveloped me.

I was eight years old when the stepfather deconstructed my childhood and constructed his wall. My grandma, my mom's Mom was his first supporter; she was my first silent witness. Night after night, the stepfather takes me from my bed; night after night, I pray someone will come save me. Momma would save me if she were here, but she isn't here; she's at work. Then one night, eyes shut tight, pinned to the bed, beneath the weight of the stepfather; I open my eyes. Not sure why; I never opened them before. I turn my head toward the bedroom door; it's slightly ajar. Someone's standing in the hallway watching—it's grandma. Several years later I pondered; did the stepfather leave the door ajar on purpose? Did he know grandma was watching? How long had grandma known? How many times had she watched?

As I lay there watching Grandma watching me, listening to the stepfather's huffing and puffing, I try to recall what awful thing I must have done to make the stepfather hurt me, and Grandma, not want, to help me. Night after night I cry myself to sleep. Until one night I don't. No more tears. I'm cried out. Fast-forward, I'm eleven years old; no longer a child. I know I'm not a child because I have no memories of being a child. I no longer wonder. I no longer worry. I no longer care. Why wonder, worry, or care about something that will never change. Grandma was my first silent witness. Sadly, she's not my last. Many come, many see, many hear. All remain silent.

When I was six-years-old my first wall builder/my dad, designed and built me a prison wall of pain and shame atop a four-year foundation of tears and fears. When I was eight-years-old, my second wall builder; the stepfather came to live with us. Within six months he redesigned daddy's prison wall and secured the foundation with more tears and fears. Five wall builders followed each adding their personal touch to daddy's original design. November 8, 2016; in three months I'll be sixty-seven-years-old. My past and in-between scurry into my present. My eighth-wall builder; my president, wants to build a prison/border wall. Imprisoning those within; keeping those in need of hope and help, who don't look, think or believe as he does—out! The three most powerful, most influential men in my life; my father, the stepfather, and my president. Three trusted heads of households. My biological father presided over a family of 4; from a Rickety house in Birmingham Alabama. The stepfather presided over a family of 8; from a two-family flat in Detroit, Michigan; my commander and chief; the President of the United States of America, presides over a family of more than 328 million; from White House, in Washington D.C. Three different men, three different ages, and three different body types from three different walks of life. Three men, who swore to honor and fulfill their duties as head of household; three men, who swore to serve, protect, and defend the families entrusted into their care; three men with no physical similarities; three fraudulent men with the same immoral character.

Immorality has one objective. That objective is to feed; to devour humanity; to gorge itself on our hate, anger, greed, prejudice, indifference, hurt, pain, and shame. It has no preference, no likes or dislikes; its human disregard spans the globe, covets every nation and every nationality. No one is exempt; it is gender blind, age blind, status blind, and color blind. To be human—sinners saved by grace dictates; we cannot eradicate immorality. However, should we *choose* to embrace our collective purpose; *choose* to acknowledge; we *are* the church; we *are* the Body of Christ. Should we *choose* to be united—*one* people under God—*choose* to stop feeding immorality; we can *collectively* weaken its influence and loosen its grip. Likewise, should we *choose* to disregard our collective purpose; *choose* to remain divided; *choose* to continue feeding immorality; we *collectively* strengthen its influence and tighten its grip. Evil will continue to put down roots, continue to grow, continue to thrive, continue to spread, continue to divide; continue to separate.

Evil prides itself on having done what we humans appear incapable of doing—see God's truth amid the world's lies. See ourselves as equals, brothers and sisters, endowed by our Creator, appointed the same rights, privileges, liberties, and freedoms. Evil has no human prejudices, no human weaknesses, no human frailties, and no human preferences. Evil views all humans the same. When evil looks at us it sees one thing—it sees nourishment/food/fuel. Evil can't do anything to us, without us. He needs loyal, indifferent, self-absorbed followers of like mind and character; a pimp/womanizer, a steelworker/child-molester, and a condescending, United States President—*build that wall!*

Childhood

I'm not a very sociable child, don't much care for anyone's company other than my own. People say I'm different, peculiar. No one wants to be around me. I make them uncomfortable, and I'm totally okay with that. But there's a serious downside to being seen as different; it gives people the excuse they need not to get involved. I live in a house masquerading as a home, surrounded by people disguised as family, imprisoned behind a brick wall of molestation, cemented in shame and fear built by a man who somehow convinced an entire household, including me, he was the best thing that ever happened to us.

It doesn't take me long to realize, the man living in our house insisting I call him Daddy isn't the man he's pretending to be, but no one "seems" to see that other than me. My peculiarity, coupled with the stepfather's charisma, gives people the excuse they need *not* to see. I see a prison wall; they see a barrier of protection. I see a wolf in sheep's clothing; they see a knight in shining armor. I see a predator; they see a hero. I see a liar and a cheat; they see a man trying his level best to be the father I never had. I see a disgusting, evil man. They see an unruly, ungrateful child.

When the stepfather announces he's taking me to the corner store for ice cream, everyone smiles and says how caring he is; they don't see the stops we make on the side of the road; they don't ask why it took so long for us to get back. When he sits me on his knee, every-one smiles adorningly; they don't seem to notice the sports jacket lying across his lap. When I try to pull away, family and friends call me selfish and unappreciative. They don't appear to notice the smug smile etched across the stepfather's face? No one challenges him, no one confronts him, no one questions him, no one speaks up on my behalf. No one comes to my rescue.

The more the stepfather gets away with the more brazen he becomes. The more he reveals his true character, the more excuses people make for him. The more frequent his nightly visits become, the more withdrawn I become. I think about hurting myself all the time. I can't stay this way. If I stay this way, I'm gonna die. The only way for me to save me is to become someone else. Someone who can handle shame, humiliation, and pain, and so I become someone else, someone brave and strong. Soon there will be nothing left of me, nothing left of the girl I've come to despise. I'm disappearing, but no one seems to notice. How can they notice what they never saw? I'm different; people don't like different. People don't trust different; people are afraid of different.

The stepfather brags about his exploits to anyone willing to listen. He brags and boasts about all the things he's gotten away with and how he can get people to do pretty much anything he wants. Those he brags to think he's talking about someone else, they don't realize he's talking about them, laughing at them. I'm eleven and I see what he's doing; they're grown men and women. Why can't they see? Are they blind? What's wrong with them?

The stepfather might not have booksmarts, but he knows how to read people. He knows the proud, selfish, greedy, fearful, and longing, are easily distracted. He knows who'll turn a blind eye, who'll defend him to the end rather than admit they were wrong or risk losing what he's promised. He knows who will go along to get along, and those who don't care one way or the other as long as they get rewarded for their complacency. He's a trickster, an illusionist. People see what they want to see, hear what they want to hear. He mesmerizes the wicked, polarizes the uncertain, dominates the fearful, and distracts the righteous. Family, friends, and neighbors call him *the man*—the man with the know-how, the man with the good job, the man with the money.

The stepfather is the one everybody goes to when they need some chump change or small loan. He provides the weekend entertainment—the gambling tables, music, cold beer, hard liquor, fried chicken, and catfish sandwiches. Mom cooks and collects the money. The fact that he charges interest on his loans; restaurant prices for the food, beer, and liquor; and takes a hefty percentage of each player's winnings doesn't seem to bother anyone. Nothing he does seems to bother anyone; he's the man. I soon realize people care more about money, food, and alcohol than they'll ever care about me. I determine and accept I'm on my own. No one is coming to my rescue. I would try to recuse myself, but I don't exist.

Then one day, out of the blue, the stepfather says if I tell my mom what he's doing, she'll put me out. When I ask him why, he replies, "Because she loves me, hates yo no-account daddy, and you just like him."

My first thought, if mom hates my dad and I'm just like him, she must hate me too. The stepfather leans down, places his finger under my chin, tilts my head upward, and grins. His face is so big, and his breath smells. The only thing I see is his Pall Mall tobacco-stained teeth. I don't know how, but he always seems to know what I'm thinking, and that terrifies me. If mom kicks me out, where will I go? The fact that I'm only eleven never enters my mind. I decide not to chance it; I kept my head down, my mouth shut, and try to avoid him as much as possible. Mom notices I'm always walking with my head down and shouts, "Girl! Stop walking around looking at the floor. One day you gonna walk into a wall or fall, and bust yo head wide open!"

I want to tell Mom why I don't look up anymore, but whenever I look up, the stepfather's always there, standing by her side. His words echo in my ears, "You just like yo no-account daddy. If you tell yo momma, she gonna put you out."

My biological father and the stepfather, don't look alike but they're exactly, the same. They both profit from the misery, pain, fear, and suffering of others. Their primary differences, my biological father pimps desperate, fearful women; the stepfather pimp's desperate families and poor neighborhoods. My biological father has one stream of income; the stepfather has multiple streams of income. My biological father thinks short term; the stepfather thinks long term. My biological father only thinks about the present; the stepfather thinks about the present in relation to the future. My father spends; the stepfather invests.

We live in a poor neighborhood. I really hate living here. The stepfather has more than enough money to move us to a better neighborhood, but there's no chance of that ever happening. If we moved to a better neighborhood, he wouldn't have any control; he wouldn't be able to manipulate educated, financially secure people. He also knows the possibility of those he leaves behind; his robot followers, coming to the suburbs to visit; is *never*! Not to mention, with fewer people in the house, I might actually get noticed.

Most of the women in our neighborhood are on welfare; most everyone else is unemployed. Those fortunate enough to have jobs work under the table so they don't have to pay taxes. The stepfather is one of the few men living in the neighborhood with a legit job, nice car, and a bank account. When he isn't hustling or hosting gambling parties, he works at Great Lakes Steel. This makes him a big deal throughout the neighborhood. He's always there to lend a [helping] hand to the poor and those in-between jobs. Not because he cares, but because, their scared and desperate; and scared, desperate people are valuable, easily led commodities. In the end, they will pay him back, far more than they borrowed.

My biological father and the stepfather bring pain and misery to everyone they touch. Not once does either consider the devastation and destruction they're causing. When I look at President Trump, I see my biological father and the stepfather—three pimps, constantly on the lookout, for someone/something to pimp. My biological father pimped desperate, fearful women. The stepfather pimped desperate families. My commander in chief pimps desperate nations. Three different men, three different streams of financial revenue, all pimps, all skilled in the art of persuasion. Attentive listeners, expert observers, pathological liars, and skilled manipulators. Endowed with the ability to seduce their prey into revealing their innermost thoughts, secrets, desires, and fears and afterward convincing them the choices they were manipulated into making were their own. Those of us who fall victim to their manipulation rarely realize what we've done to ourselves until it's too late. Why? We live in desperate times.

So intent on getting what we "think" belongs to us. What we "think" was taken from us. What we "think" we want. What we "think" we need. What we "think" we deserve. Beliving it's okay to take back what we "think" rightfully belongs to us, what we "think" was stolen from us—by whatever means necessary. No matter the cost, no matter the loss, no matter who gets hurt. What we fail to realize—not only have we provided the wall builder with bricks and mortar to wall others out; we've also provided him with bricks and mortar to wall us in.

What we do to others externally, we do to ourselves internally. The more walls we build, the more apathetic we become. The more apathetic we become, the more divided we become. The more divided we become, the more segregated we become. The more segregated we become, the more we invite evil into our lives. The more we invite evil into our lives, the more we invite God out of our lives. The more we invite God out of our lives, the more we imprison ourselves. Those walled out aren't the wall builder's ultimate pray; those walled in are. When Mr. Trump looks at us; we the people; the United States of America; the Soul of America, he sees his crowning glory, his ultimate sale, his greatest commission—his con of a lifetime.

When I was a child, my innocence was sacrificed for money and creature comforts. My ugly, inconvenient truth was traded for the stepfather's convenient lies and false promises. Those entrusted with my care and safety stood silent as I was raped and abused. I see the same rape and abuse happening throughout America today. I see we the people allowing our nation to be raped and abused by prejudice, hate, and inequality. I see that rape, abuse, prejudice, hate, and inequality turning back the hands of time. I see those of us proclaiming ourselves "good" hiding in the shadows, peaking through cracks; murmuring, complaining, and shaking our heads in disbelief. Yet, unwilling to step up or speak out against the inhumanity of injustice. If not for grace and mercy, where would we be? I shudder to think.

Should we choose to close our borders, we close our hearts to God's heart's desire—Eternal life for His children, and we open them to Satan's hunger—Eternal death for God's children.

The Body of Evil, the Salesman, the Mantle, and the Covenant

Some of us believe hate put Donald Trump in the Oval Office. I believe, believing otherwise is far too troubling for us to think about, let alone consider. Yes, hate played a part in the 2016 presidential election, but it received a great deal of help from both unlikely and unwitting sources. Evil is one body comprised of many limbs/facets. Of all its limbs hate has proven the most valuable and productive. Working in concert with other limbs (i.e., anger, jealousy, greed, envy, etcetera) Hate has grown and spread the body of evil in ways never imagined or considered. Evil would have us believe he's hypothetical, random, a science fiction movie or television show, something man made up, a figment of the imagination. He isn't any of those things! He reasons, calculates, surmises, feeds, and defecates. He is immorally driven and task-orientated. He has one goal—human annihilation! Under his influence—by our hands. He is evil personified; the head of the snake; the embodiment of sin.

Evil realized early on hate alone; would not win the 2016 election; unleashing his entire arsenal of dysfunction upon us would not win him the election. Why? Because evil knows what many of us have yet to realize—that there are far more of us who love than those of us who hate. Evil simply didn't have the numbers it needed to win. It needed help; it needed to get the negative word out; it needed to turn up the heat; stir stuff up. It went after the broken, suffering, unemployed, scared, hungry, disadvantaged, and disenfranchised. Troubled individuals looking for a way out, suddenly found themselves caught up in evil's web of greed and indifference—due to unforeseen circumstances. Evil can't move from place to place on its own; it can't spread itself or duplicate itself. It needs us for that. We are the catalyst for every good thing and every bad thing. Nothing moves, nothing spreads, nothing duplicates without us.

Evil concludes the 2016 presidential primaries are its best shot at turning the political tide in its favor. Thus far, hate has been evil's largest campaign contributor; it also has the most base voters. Evil orders hate to increase its base; to find, capture, and persuade the minds of those who believe ourselves to be good, fair, honest, kind, and just, but now find ourselves treading-water, robbing peter to pay paul, unemployed, unable to provide for our families; angry, scared and disillusioned. Our minds wander into unfamiliar, forbidden places. We find ourselves entertaining thoughts we never had before. Hate knows exactly who we are, but before it can finish changing us into who we're not; it must first change how we envision ourselves to be; it must change how we envision hate. Hate changes its MO (Modus Operandi) into something more appealing. Something that seems kind, concerned, and empathic. Something that justifies wrong behavior—under certain circumstances. Evil delegates hate a measure of time to turn the political tide in his favor. Allowing hate to step away from the chaos it already wrought, now in full swing and self-sustaining.

Hate's new voter demographics: those of us who perceive ourselves kind, caring, and decent but now find ourselves conflicted, hurting, emotionally exhausted, and physically drained. Why would hate go after those who are conflicted and hurting? Because hate knows conflicted, hurting people are desperate people. Desperate people looking for a way out of the conflict, looking for a way to ease the hurt, looking for someone, something to blame. Hence, the sad but true phrase "hurt people hurt people."

Hate painted a bull's-eye on our backs and threw darts at our emotions, magnifying, manipulating and distorting our hurt, disappointment, fear, anger, pain, frustration, despair, and desire to hurt those who hurt us—the United States government. The hurt and conflicted, were the voters hate needed to sway—to turn the political tide in evil's favor. Those of us hurting just enough; conflicted just enough; angry just enough to be persuaded; to do wrong for the right reason. Persuaded to do wrong for "our" greater "individual" good. In accordance, with the world, above all persons and things— Self-Preservation. Persuaded into and doing bad for a greater good, that greater good being us. What better way to satisfy and ease our hurt and resolve our conflict than voting for someone of Mr. Trump's questionable character, someone controversial and argumentative. Someone who didn't care, someone who would do and say the things we wanted to do and say but couldn't.

We voted a man known worldwide for his bias, cruelty, greed, and selfishness into the highest office on earth for the satisfaction of giving the United States government the middle finger and shouting, "Screw you!" My mom called that kind of reasoning cutting off your nose to spite your face. Hate enticed us, hate influenced us, hate encouraged us, hate motivated us, but hate did not choose for us; we chose for ourselves. We chose to become hurt people who hurt people. Evil doesn't have the power or the authority to make us do or say anything we don't want to do or say. We gave evil power and authority when we chose vengeance over one another.

Some of us were so fed up with the status quo of politics we didn't even bother to vote. What we failed to realize until it was too late is that there is no such thing as not voting. By not exercising our right to vote, we inadvertently voted for the very person or thing we chose not to vote for. Others of us, despite our distrust of the male presidential candidates, felt voting for the female candidate was completely out of the question, given those "female emotional tendencies".

Last but not least, there was those of us who were just sick and tired of being sick and tired—sick and tired of the lies, sick and tired of not being able to make ends meet, sick and tired of being unemployed, sick and tired of being hungry, sick and tired of holes in the soles of our shoes and the holes in our souls, sick and tired of low wages and high taxes, sick and tired of foreigners crossing the border and taking our jobs (jobs we didn't want because they weren't good of us yet were too good for foreigners). We kicked, screamed, and cried!

We didn't want foreigners coming into America taking our jobs. Did I mention—jobs we did not want? Why would we put so much time, effort, and energy into something we did not want? So much effort into not helping those in need?

The best job I had during my years of employment was educational sales. Not only was I good at it; I helped a lot of people change their lives and made a lot of money doing it. I loved selling; it made me feel good about myself, and for the first time in my life, I "thought" I knew what it meant to be happy. My mom used to say, my sister, brother, and I had the gift of gab like our dad. Not the best pep talk for mom to give us kids considering Dad was a narcissist, egotistical womanizing pimp. That aside, I honestly believe the ability to sell, the talent to speak easily, and confidently when used for good is an amazing, inspirational gift. I also believe the ability to sell when used for evil is a lethal demoralizing weapon.

Not once during the three years, I watched and listened to Mr. Trump, did I see a President; Commander-in-Chief. Not once did I see or hear empathy, honesty, integrity, or commitment. Not once did I see him use his powers of persuasion/selling for the good of anyone other than himself. Not once did I see or hear a man who loved his country, its citizens, nor anyone else other than himself. What I saw and heard was a salesman at his lethal demoralizing best. What I saw and heard was, a man constantly selling and working the crowd, a man continually looking for ways of getting more, consistently subtracting from others and adding to himself. Not because he needed more but because he wanted more. Because no matter how much he has, no matter how much is given to him, no matter how much he takes from others, it will never be enough. I saw a man addicted to power and chaos. I listened to him advocate hate, bigotry, separatism, and division with ease and confidence. I saw a mortal man place himself above other humans, above the laws of man and above the laws of God. I saw a man with no respect for human life, a man who saw humans as revenue; stockpiled commodities to be bartered, traded, bought and sold pursuant to his whims and indiscretions.

And I saw us, we the people, trusting and believing indiscriminately without forethought.

Mr. Trump told women, "I have no respect for you."

To which we replied, "That's okay, we'll vote for you anyway."

He told people of color, "I have no respect for you."

To which we replied, "That's okay, we'll vote for you anyway."

He told Christians and believers, by way of his words, actions, and deeds, "I have no respect for you or your God."

To which we replied, "That's okay, we'll vote for you anyway."

I accredit Mr. Trump with one truth, and that truth is this—he told us exactly who he was. He demonstrated time and time again throughout his entire presidential campaign, "This is who I am, I will *not* change!"

He never lied about who he was. He never hid his character or what he believed in. To which we replied, "That's okay! We'll vote for you anyway."

That being said, the 2016 presidential election was more about emotion than anything else. Two candidates stood before us; one male and one female. For many of us torn between the two our emotions elected Mr. Trump the better candidate. Mr. Trump was elected president of the United States because of our feelings—our hurt, fear, anger, disappointment, frustration, and, yes, our hate. He was elected because of our unwillingness to think or love outside ourselves; our unwillingness to rise above the hurt, anger, disappointment, frustration, and hate; our refusal to see and hear what Mr. Trump so proudly shouted, and arrogantly demonstrated time and time again, "This is who I am, I will *never* change! I don't care about anyone or anything but myself!"

To which we replied, "That's okay! We'll vote for you anyway."

Mr. Trump is a salesman. A good salesman sees the benefit of an asset as well as the benefit of a liability. Good salesmen also know the importance of timing—when, where, and how to best utilize an asset/liability to their advantage. Mr. Trump didn't try to hide who he was, what he was, or what he stood for because he didn't have to. All he had to do was observe the lay of the land/nation, gauge the emotional temperature of the people, watch, listen, and wait, therein uncovering what many American voters refused to see hidden in plain sight. That the mental state of the American nation suggested Mr. Trump's bias, destructive, outlandish behavior would work to his advantage not only during the presidential primaries but throughout the presidential election as well.

Mr. Trump did what an experienced salesman does. He weighed, considered, and determined what was best for him; giving no thought to the American people. He sold us on what he determined we wanted to hear—a "calculated" solution to our anger, fear, hurt, pain, and disappointment. He sold us on a crumbling America; that only he could make great again; convinced us that he deserved our honor; that he possessed the power, the glory, and the greatness, to restore America to her former greatness. And yet…

"You are worthy, our Lord and God, to receive glory and honor and power, for You created all things, and by Your will, they were created and have their being." Revelations 4:11

Can a man, created by God do what only his Creator can? God birthed America. God nurtured America. God grew America. God empowered America. That she might, in turn, nurture, grow and empower less fortunate nations. Hence, only God can restore what America has lost. America's nationwide repentance compels worldwide restoration. How is that possible. There's a famous quote that says, *"The eyes are the window to the soul."* On July 4, 1776, God, favored America to lead—by example. To be a Light of Help and Hope to the nations. Praytell, brothers, and sisters, what do We the People suppose; the Eyes of the nations see; when looking at you and I—the Soul of America?

Somewhere along the way—We the People exchanged America's declaration of human equality, freedom, and liberty, for a red, white, and blue, fireworks celebration of Bar-B-Q ribs, chicken, hamburgers, hot dogs, chips, potato salad, coleslaw, cold beer, and soda pop; exchanged our Armor of Honor, Help, and Hope for garments of selfish-indifference. Why, would we do such a thing? Why, would we forfeit the Greater Godly Things that made America great; for the ungodly things that lessen, divide, separate, and destroy? If we do not question the source of our behavior; who/what is influencing us? Who/what is motivating us? Who/what we are granting access to our soul/emotions? If we do not diligently seek the truth; the source prompting our behavior; our behavior/we have no reason to change.

Mr. Trump told us what we "thought" we wanted to hear; not what we needed to hear. *Emotional Blackmail!* He sold us on American superiority; our right to be fearful, angry, selfish, indifferent people; a nation divided rather than a nation united. We became transfixed with the fantasy of *me*, severing ourselves from the actuality of *we*—being of service to one another. We allowed ourselves to be spoon-fed pleasant, convenient lies because we were sick and tired of being force-fed unpleasant, inconvenient truths. Mr. Trump gave us permission to hate, fear, and disrespect ourselves in lieu of ourselves.

Two very important lessons I've learned over the years: wrongs spoken can't be unspoken and wrongs done can't be undone. The best thing I can do for myself and others is to learn from my mistakes and pass that knowledge on. Not learning from our mistakes is the true tragedy of a mistake. Our inability to help others due to a lack of knowledge is equally tragic. God knows many things about us, but the most precious thing He knows is our heart. His spirit, His love, His goodness, His forgiveness, His grace, and His mercy resonate amid every resounding heartbeat. He knows all there is to know about us. He has known all there is to know since before our beginning. That being said, yesterday is dead and gone, and tomorrow has yet to arrive. Today is the most important day of our lives. Today is our new beginning. Today is another chance for us to get it right! We owe it to ourselves to give ourselves another chance to get it right!

Regardless of the "seeming hopelessness" of it all, there's a constant upside to our every downside. That upside is God. He knows everything there is to know. He knew what we were going to think before we thought it. He knew what we were going to say before we said it; the words we will ultimately speak. God stood amid our past, before it became past, and amid our future, eons before it arrived.

Everything we need to navigate the ever-changing winds of this life is anchored within us. God knows these things about us because He hid these things within us. Mistakes/bad choices are merely opportunities waiting to be recognized.

We are positive and negative, good and bad. Mr. Trump exploited our negative, our bad, our hurt, anger, fear, disappointment, frustration, hate and need for revenge. Why? Because he knew our emotions/feelings were the keys, the keys he needed to open the floodgates and secure his social posturing within the political arena. And though it pains me to say this, we needed Mr. Trump as much as he needed us. We needed him because he was our best shot at sticking it to the government, making them hurt the way they made us hurt over the years. He would burst their political bubble the same way they busted our livelihood bubble without warning, without regard, without regret! On Tuesday, November 8, 2016, we took our hurt, fear, anger, disappointment, frustration, and vindictiveness into the voting booth and voted our emotions/feelings. With one flick of the pen, we elected Donald Trump our champion and avenger, without forethought, without regard, without regret.

Yes, a small portion of us voted our hate, but the majority of us voted our hurt, fear, anger, disappointment, frustration, lack, and need for revenge. We voted the hell away with everyone else. Time to look out for number one; time to look out for me. Thing is, there is no *me*, without *we*, just as there is no, *we* without *me*. God designed every language known and unknown. Why of all the words God designed did He choose to make *we* right side up and *me* right side down? Why would He do such a thing? How about this, God is no respecter of persons. God created us equal. God created us joint heirs. God created none of us less or more, none of us higher or lower than the other. Hence, there is no me; there is only we.

Mr. Trump's presidential run was a salesman's dream—millions of broken human commodities, potential human revenue caught up in his wave of self-glorification, clamoring for his attention, hanging onto his every word; his for the taking. He didn't need us, he never envisioned himself actually winning the election. It was all entertainment an extension of his reality show; only this time he wasn't standing on a television stage. He was standing on the world stage, auditioning to become the greatest reality star of all time, president of the United States of America. Even after winning the Republican nomination, Mr. Trump remained skeptical, concluding win or lose, it was a win-win for him. At the very least, he was assured worldwide recognition, which would go a long way in securing future monetary ventures.

President Trump fancies himself a human ringmaster, considers certain races of people beneath him, believes he's not only better but smarter than humankind; society as a whole existing solely for his entertainment and pleasure. Deeming some of us less than others; collateral damage; an acceptable loss. Truth be told, Mr. Trump, having judged "some" of us less deserving than others didn't matter one way or the other. After all, was said and done he saw us all the same. Collateral damage. Acceptable losses. A means to his end; his legacy. What did Mr. Trump see when he looked at us? He saw all the hurting, fearful, vindictive, broken human commodities, he gathered along the way, in hopes of procuring the greatest sales commission of his lifetime—the dehumanization of the United States of America.

Yes, he actually believes he can do that. Why? Because he thinks so highly of himself and so lowly of us. Mr. Trump wants four more years in the White House. Why? To secure his legacy as the most controversial, corrupt president in US history? Future generations be damned! Thing is, he can't get reelected without the majority of us. Thing is, he believes he can. Why? Because he believes there are more of us who hate than those of us who love! More of us who take than give! More of us who cower than challenge! More of us who mummer and complain in the shadows of unrighteousness than stand up and shout in the glare of righteousness! Mr. Trump doesn't want four more years for the good of the nation; he wants four more years for the good of himself. We are his once in a lifetime—art of the sale! His greatest deception. Somewhere along the way, Mr. Trump determined he was more deserving than other humans, determined he deserves everything this world has to offer, as well as everything it doesn't have to offer. Monetary compensation no longer satisfies Mr. Trump; human compensation is the only thing he considers worthy of his wheeling and dealing.

Being a salesman, Mr. Trump knew, given time, we would tell him exactly what he needed to say to get us to buy what he was selling. Three years later, some of us are still agonizing over the decision we made on Tuesday, November 8, 2016. Others of us continue to justify and celebrate the choice we made that day, while others of us continue to blame our actions on the actions of others; the government made us do it. Last but not least, there are those of us who just don't care anymore; don't believe things will ever get better; have lost hope in us as a people and a nation; seeing nothing but greed, lies, betrayal, and corruption around every corner. I, however, know, beyond a shadow of a doubt; there is more good in us than bad.

America's history has shown us time and time again when we're at our worse, we rise! When all seems lost; we rise! When other nations count us out, we rise! As we rose and overcame past evils, so shall we rise and overcome this present evil. The only thing expected of— We the American people. That we return the Mantle of Sanctuary entrusted to us by the Founding Fathers to its rightful place—the multihued; multiethnic; multicultural shoulders of the American nation. Only by returning the Sanctuary Mantle to its rightful place can America continue receiving God's favor. The Founding Fathers; having acquired knowledge, wisdom, and understanding—by virtue, of the Holy Spirit; did unitedly declare—We the American nation!— our brothers/sisters keeper; domestic and foreign; within our borders, on the outskirts of our borders, and beyond our borders! That we, the American nation should serve as a symbol of Hope, Help, and a Future. That we, the American nation will *"always"* extend Human Kindness and Courtesy to *"all"* in need of help. Without bias! Without exception! Without exclusion! We promise…

> *[a]bove all things, we will love one another, be kind and humble to one another, carry one another's burden with love, patience, and understanding,*

expecting nothing in return and love our neighbor as ourselves. The same law applies to the native-born and the foreigner residing among us. We will not oppress or mistreat a foreigner for we ourselves were once foreigners. Cursed is anyone who withholds justice from a foreigner; we will love the foreigner as ourselves. As we treat the foreigner, so shall we be treated.

We will be of one mind, having compassion for one another. We will be tenderhearted and courteous. We will not return evil for evil nor insult for insult; instead, we will repay evil with blessing, knowing this is what God called us to do; knowing we are the body of Christ, knowing the body is not supported by one of us; it is supported by all of us. Knowing we are sanctuary to the whole of humanity, not a select few. Knowing, united we stand, divided we fall, united we are strong, divided we are weak, united we are harmony, united we are peace, united we can do all things through Christ who strengthens us; a nation divided against itself will not stand. A divided people are easily conquered by the forces of evil. We will reject the factious man, after a first and second warning knowing such a man is perverted and self-condemned. We will reject those who follow such a man. We will reject the separatist and dividers.

This is the mantle America embraced. This is the mantle that decreed her a sanctuary. This is the mantle our Founding Fathers acknowledged, accepted and officially declared to be passed down to subsequent generations, that we the people might continue to inherit God's blessing. This is the mantle that granted America God's favor; favor that placed her above other nations. Not because of anything we did but because of what was done for us. This is the mantle of sanctuary that acknowledges humankind's solidarity as ordained by God.

The mantle of sanctuary that declares what God joins together, no man shall put asunder. God blessed us beyond measure to right human wrongs; to uplift and comfort; to strengthen and encourage; to defend and protect the innocent, weak, oppressed, and destitute. Of what good is such a prestigious mantle if those entrusted with it no longer perform the good works required to sustain it? A now divided, wanton, self-serving people, who elected to abandon America's confirmed; established post; in lieu of creature comforts. Of what good?

Unlike man, God is a Promise Keeper; He will reaffirm the favor America unwittingly suspended when we the people pick up the cross of responsibility we chose to lay down. The cross of responsibility acknowledged, accepted, and established on our behalf by the Founding Fathers affirming we the people of every generation—past, present, and future—do intentionally take upon ourselves the burdens and hardships of the less fortunate. Affirming we the people of every generation—past, present, and future—will *not* be intimidated nor persuaded by the prejudices of corrupt men. Affirming we the people *will,* no matter the cost, rightly, justly, and fairly uphold the original enforceable promise, acknowledged, accepted, affirmed and written upon the pages of the United States Declaration of Independence. Wherein it is written rightly, justly, and fairly on behalf of *all* people, "We hold these truths to be self-evident, that all men are created equal, that they are endowed by their Creator with certain unalienable Rights, that among these are Life, Liberty, and the pursuit of Happiness."

United we *will* turn the tide of inhumanity flooding and dividing our nation and spilling its sludge into other nations. Nations, we are mantle bond by God and country to defend and protect.

The New Covenant

Jesus said, "Do not think that I have come to abolish the Law or the Prophets; I have not come to abolish them, but to fulfill them. For I tell you truly, until heaven and earth pass away, not a single jot, not a stroke of a pen, will disappear from the Law until everything is accomplished." Matthew 5:17

All of humanity is under the New Covenant; no one is exempt. In it, God makes certain promises to His people. In return for His promises, we are expected to conduct ourselves reflective of those promises. We are expected to love one another as God loves us, treat one another as we want to be treated, and sincerely profess and declare Christ Jesus as Lord and God.

We are reconciled to God by grace alone apart from anything we do. Upon His death, Jesus purchased us that we might receive full forgiveness from sin. Justice was satisfied on the cross. Christ's forgiveness is perfect and complete. In terms of justification, God no longer remembers our sins; it's as if we never committed them. God set aside His anger, promising never to be angry with us again. The New Covenant established by Jesus is an everlasting covenant of love and peace. God qualifies us. He is our refuge and strength an ever-present help in times of trouble. Jesus is our Savior, Redeemer, and Intercessor. Nothing can separate us from the love of God. God credits us with the perfect righteousness of Christ. We did not earn righteousness; righteousness was given to us, as grace was given to us by way of Christ's sacrifice. The Holy Spirit our Comforter, Teacher, and Guide convicts; equips, empowers, and serves as a constant reminder of God's promise.

Under the New Covenant, we no longer need a priest to meditate for us; we now know the Lord for ourselves. God is for us. God justifies us; there is no condemnation. When we sin, Jesus does not judge us; He defends us. His grace empowers us. He supplies all our needs. God's favor is unearned and unmerited. He empowers us to overcome the enemy. We have God's delegated authority over demons and disease. We live under His divine protection; we are destined to reign in life. The door of the throne room is always open to us because Christ died for us. God the Father is always with us because we can approach Christ the Son with freedom and confidence. It is through Him that we are made possible. Under the Old Covenant was "to do." Under the New Covenant, it is done. All things made new; God gives us eternal life.

What does God ask in return that we might inherit His promises?

He asks that we trust in Christ Jesus. Place our life in His hands. Take the crown off our head and lay it at His feet. Choose to believe what the Bible says about Him—that He died for the sins of the world and rose victorious from the dead. Let others know He is our Redeemer and King. Ask Him to fill us with His Spirit that we might know Him more. That we might know Him better.

No Evil Is Greater Than God's Ensuing Good

As I've grown older, I have come to appreciate even during the most reprehensible times of my life; God's timing was always perfect; that reprehensible things were as they should be at those particular moments in time; that at the appointed time, soul gives way to spirit. That during those particular moments in time, I become spiritually aware; therein amassing the knowledge, wisdom, and understanding long-established in anticipation of those reprehensible things. That, at the appointed time, I possess the strength to endure, the courage to withstand, and the fearlessness to ensure the still pending arrival of God's ensuing good.

"The vision awaits its appointed time; it hastens to the end—it will not lie. If it seems slow, wait for it; it will surely come; it will not delay." Habakkuk 2:4

My Life Interpretation of the Aforementioned

No manner of evil can dissuade a vision awaiting its appointed time. What hurries in the spirit often appears slow to the soul. The vision is true; it cannot lie. What God puts in motion stays in motion; until it reaches its appointed destination. It cannot be slowed; it cannot be stopped. We must be patient. We must wait for the vision. The vision that hurries to fulfill its purpose hurries to fulfill God's purpose for us; we are the purpose of the vision.

When I was six years old, my mom, sister, brother, and I left Birmingham, Alabama, and came to Detroit, Michigan. We moved into the upper flat of a two-story house on Van Dyke Street. Sears and Roebuck department store sat on the corner of Van Dyke Street and Gratiot Avenue. The store parking lot was adjacent to the side street that ran alongside the neighborhood barbershop located next to our house. We didn't have a lot; pretty much everything was secondhand—furniture from the used furniture store; black-and-white television from the TV repair shop; clothes from acquaintances, neighbors, and friends.

That's not to say we never got new clothes. Every Christmas, we each got a Goodfellow box. My sister and I always got new dresses, usually plaid, socks, and a bag of candy. Our bother got a new shirt, a pair of pants usually navy blue or black, socks, and a bag of candy. But our best clothes came from Momma; she was an amazing seamstress. Whenever Momma had a little extra money, she would buy paper patterns; discontinued fabrics, and remnants. There wasn't a design pattern Momma couldn't follow, but she always added a special touch to make the design her own. Once momma's design recreation was complete, it looked as good as or better than the clothes displayed in fashion magazines and department store windows.

When Mom cooked, she cooked food that stretched out three or four days. As a result, we ate variations of the same meal throughout most of the week. Pinto beans, salted pork, and cornbread the first day. Pinto beans mixed with Mueller's elbow macaroni the second day. More pinto beans and elbow macaroni the third day. Cornbread and buttermilk the fourth day. There were also black-eyed peas with slimy okra and cow tongue days. Ugh! But Momma didn't just cook cow tongue for dinner. Imagine taking a cow tongue, Hostess white bread, and Miracle Whip sandwich to school for lunch. I sat in the lunchroom watching other kids laughing as they traded their baloney, salami-and-cheese, peanut butter and jelly sandwiches with one another; but no one ever wanted to trade sandwiches with me. Wonder why!

Breakfast wasn't much better: Quaker Oats grits with margarine; Quaker Oats oatmeal with margarine and powdered milk; or powdered milk and whatever cereal happened to be on sale when

Momma went to the grocery store, usually Kix cereal or Momma's homemade pancakes with margarine and Alaga syrup. Momma's pancakes or Kix cereal were my preferred choices, but there was no way of knowing what I'd be getting until I sat down at the kitchen table. And there was no negotiating Momma's meal selection; either eat what's in front of you or go without. To this day, I do not eat pinto beans, black-eyed peas, oatmeal, grits, Alaga syrup, or corn-bread and buttermilk. I do, however, eat succotash and fried okra on occasion. That being said, what I remember most about those unappetizing, boring, repetitive meals is this: Momma made sure we never went hungry.

I lived for the "every now and then" days, those days when Mom left home empty-handed and returned with bags of Hostess choc-olate cream-filled cupcakes, Twinkies, doughnuts, and cherry pies from the day-old bakery or a bag of broken cookies from Sears and Roebuck. My favorite cookies were Windmill cookies with almonds and shortbread cookies layered in marshmallows, strawberry pre-serves, and topped with shredded coconut—mouthwatering broken pieces of deliciousness. I loved broken cookie day but didn't under-stand why the cookies were always broken. When I asked momma she said, "Do you like eating one kind of cookie or lots of different cookies?"

"I like lots of different cookies," I reply.

Momma smiles and says, "Well, there you have it. I buy broken cookies so you have lots of different cookies to choose from, not just one."

Her explanation made perfect sense. Why would anyone eat one kind of cookie when they could have lots of different cookies? Momma and the lady living in the downstairs flat became friends and watched each other's kids whenever one of them needed to go to the store or run an errand. One day, Momma was getting ready to walk to Sears and Roebuck and I ask if I can please go with her, and to my surprise, she says yes. We drop my sister and brother off downstairs, walk through the backyard, down the alleyway, across the side street, through the Sears and Roebuck parking lot, into the

store, past the main floor, and down the staircase to the bargain basement. I'm seven years old and it's my first time in a department store;
to say I'm excited doesn't come close to describing what I'm feeling.
I've never been to Disneyland, but it can't possibly be better than
this. Everywhere I look is magical and alive with color! I feel like I'm
gonna bust! The people who buy this stuff must be rich!

As Momma and I step from the staircase onto the bargain-base-
ment floor, all the magic of the main floor fades away. Nothing magical down here, just bargain tables with big on-sale and discontinued
items signs. Momma takes hold of my hand and heads for the discontinued fabrics table. As she rummages through the various pieces
of cloth, I can't help noticing the angry woman standing on the far
side of the basement glaring at us. Why is she so angry? Had me
and Momma done something not on purpose that upset her? I tug
Momma's dress. She looks down at me, then looks in the direction
I'm staring. She doesn't say anything, just places her open hand on
top of my head, gently turns my face in the opposite direction, and
continues rummaging through the fabrics.

Not finding anything she likes, Momma takes my hand, and
we walk back to the staircase. I can feel the angry lady looking at us.
I turn my head to look back. Mom tightens her grip and maneuvers
me up the staircase to the main floor. There are a lot more people
in the store than when we first arrived. I take a quick look around.
What happened to all the magic? All I see is angry female faces, but
theirs aren't the only angry faces I see; their children are just as angry
as they are. Hiding behind their mother's dresses, pointing their fingers and sticking out their tongues as Mom and me walk by. Why
aren't their moms saying anything? Why don't they make their kids
stop? If I did that, Momma would snatch me up, with everybody
watching and pop my butt! But all my curiosity disappears as we near
the cookie counter. Cookies!

I wiggle myself free from Momma's grip and take off for the
cookie counter. Excited once more and grinning from ear to ear, I
look up at the tall, slender, pinked-faced man standing behind the
counter dressed in a white shirt, black pants and long white pocket

apron with matching head cap. I don't know if I was going to say something to the man or not; I only know the look on his face stopped me dead in my tracks. But now I'm confused. He's a man; why does he look exactly like the angry mothers and their angry kids? Though Momma and I are the first to arrive at the cookie counter, we're the last to be waited on. As more and more people arrive, the cookie man motions Momma to step aside, which she does. Once the cookie man gets around to waiting on Momma, he snaps at her, tells her to hurry up; he doesn't have all day. In the middle of Momma telling him she wants three dollars' worth of broken cookies, a lady walks up with a little girl. The lady, the little girl, and the cookie man look at Momma and burst out laughing. The cookie man shrugs his shoulders, shakes his head in annoyance, scoops up the broken cookies, weighs them, pours them in a bag, and hands the bag to Momma. Momma pays him, and we head for the nearest exit. I could still hear the cookie man, the lady, and the little girl laughing as we're walking away. On the way home, I ask Momma why the people in the store didn't like us.

She says, "Sometimes people just do and say mean things. I doubt they even know why they don't like us."

"But what about the kids' momma? Do they know?" I ask.

Momma stops walking, stoops down, looks me in my eyes and says, "It's not the kids, Toni, it's the parents. I don't blame the kids for how they act. I blame their parents."

"But, Momma, if I did that, you would whop me."

Momma sees I'm confused, so she repeats what she said differently, "I raised you different. You know not to act like that. Children learn from their moms and dads. They copy what their parents do because they been raised to think what their parents are doing and saying is okay. Okay, little girl, enough about that. Let's get home and eat some of these yummy cookies." Mom laughs.

Momma never mentioned that day again, and to the best of my knowledge, never told anyone about it. But at the time, I remember wondering if us being poor and having dark skin might be the reason the people in the store didn't like us. I was dark skinned and dark eyed like Momma, whereas my sister and brother were light skinned and light eyed like Daddy's family. It seemed to me everyone, not just the people at Sears and Roebuck, liked light-skinned, light-eye people better. For as long as I could remember, relatives on both sides of my family, both light skinned and dark skinned, treated my sister and brother differently than me. I always felt the difference, but before that day, at Sears and Roebuck, I never gave it serious thought when it came to family. But after that day, I saw everyone differently, my family included.

I recall the day Momma dropped me and my sister off at Daddy's momma house. Grandma Maggie greets us at the back door with a big smile on her face and ushers us into the kitchen, but once Momma leaves, so does her smile. She asks my sister if she'd like some candy; we nod our heads yes. Grandma motions us into the dining room. Sitting in the middle of her shiny Mahogany dining table is a crystal candy bowl filled with candy. She removes the top from the candy bowl and extends it to my sister. My sister reaches in and pulls out a fist full of candy, but when I reach for the candy bowl, Grandma smacks my hand away. Grandma points her finger toward the living room and tells my sister to have a seat on her plastic-covered gold French-provincial couch.

Grandma doesn't acknowledge me so I go back into the kitchen and sit down at the kitchen table, which is where I'm sitting when Momma returns a couple of hours later to pick us up. I never told Momma what Grandma did. Strangely enough, neither did my sister. The uncomfortable feelings I shrugged off when I was around certain family members, before that day at Sears and Roebuck, hurt too much to accept about my silky-haired, grey-eyed grandma, before sitting alone in her kitchen waiting for momma to come; listening to her laughing and playing with my light-skinned, hazel-eyed sister in the living room; grabbed hold of me and refused to let go. I remember that day like it was yesterday. That was the day I began my six-year prayer ritual. "God, please make my skin lighter so people will like me," I remember thinking, as I prayed, daddy and his momma had to be the meanest people on the planet—but I was wrong.

Momma's momma and the stepfather were coming. Insult to injury, by age thirteen my skin tone will be as light as my sister and brother's skin. More insult to injury—it won't make a bit of difference. I got so many mixed messages when I was a kid about skin-color. What it meant to be colored. What it meant to be light-skinned, what it meant to be dark-skinned, what it meant to be white. contradictory messages streamed in from everywhere; family, friends, neighbors, church, school, stores, television commercials, billboards—the Coppertone baby.

When I was eight years old, Momma met someone and her life blossomed, whereas my life crumbled into pieces. Three years later, I realize situations don't change until those involved change. Yet oftentimes, those involved don't change because they're waiting for the situation to change, and those aware of the situation but aren't affected by the situation don't think they should get involved or don't care enough to get involved, and therefore nothing changes. My only hope of surviving childhood is to grow up mentally. What I couldn't control physically, I could escape mentally.

When I turned eleven, I recognized the true character of my enemy, I was now able to calculate the timing of his attacks, giving myself plenty of time to take myself out of harm's way and retreat to my secret imaginary place. But I was too broken to sense the Spirit of God residing in me. I was too broken to grasp the concept of God's goodness; too broken to understand broken souls, like broken cookies, are still lovely and full of flavor; too broken to realize to be broken by man is to be gathered up by Christ, empowered by the Holy Spirit, and restored by God.

When I was eight years old, I was reprehensively broken. When I turned eleven, I recognized the methods of the enemy, but I'm still too young to defend myself, still too young to change myself, still too young to change my situation, still too young and terrified to ask for help. So I did what children do; I waited for those older than me to come to my rescue. I waited for those involved in the situation to change the situation. I waited for the situation to change itself. I waited for those not involved in to get involved. I waited for those not affected by the situation to get affected and get involved. I waited for those who didn't care to care. I waited for those who knew but pretended not to know to step up and speak out. I waited and waited and waited; nothing changed. Those who could save me had no regard for me.

*****

Eleven months into Mr. Trump's presidency, women began stepping forward and exposing "world-endorsed" supposed prestigious men who sexually abused and/or sexually assaulted them. My eyes are glued to the television screen. I watch intently as woman after woman steps onto the podium, stand steadfast behind the microphone, look directly into TV cameras, breathe in and hauntingly breathe out the horrific things they were forced to endure. As I watch and listen to these courageous, unflinching, resilient women, no longer victims, no longer afraid, no longer hushed by shame and fear, I find myself filling with pride. They are me! We are one another! I'm eight years old—again. I bow my head in empathetic solidarity, lift my hands to the ceiling, and whisper, "Me too."

I later learn, Tarana Burke, a civil rights activist from the Bronx, New York, founded the Me Too movement in 2006 and coined the term "Me Too" to raise awareness regarding widespread sexual abuse and sexual assault. Eleven years later, the #MeToo movement is born. Eleven months into Mr. Trump's presidency, Me Too/#MeToo comes full circle. Remember what I asked you to remember regarding the number 11 some pages back? That in accordance, with scripture; 11 symbolizes, disorder, chaos, and judgment. In 2006 civil rights activist Tarana Burke founded MeToo to help other women with similar experiences stand up for themselves. As Tarana tried to shine a light on the horrific sexual acts being committed against women; discord and chaos hid in the shadows; watching, waiting, and thriving. Eleven years later; eleven months into Mr. Trump's presidency Judgment arrives at its appointed time to right the wrongs discord and chaos wrought. #MeToo breaths new life into MeToo. Rich and powerful rapists, molesters, and abusers; thought to be untouchable are publicly humiliated, brought to justice and their knees; as the world watches. Wherein darkness, discord, and chaos dwell; the Light of Judgment abides and prevails; at its appointed time; in its appointed season.

"Nothing is hidden except for the purpose of having it revealed, and nothing is secret except for the purpose of having it come to light." Mark 4:22

11 years; 11 months=22. According to scripture, twenty-two symbolizes; discord, chaos, and judgment; a concentration of dis-organization. 11 years; 11 months into Mr. Trump's presidency; MeToo and #MeToo merge in unity and solidarity; exposing a past/present evil. A concentration of disorganization; discord, and chaos. Accompanied by Justice; in hot pursuit. I for one have never believed in coincidence nor happenstance. Every injustice shall be exposed by justice. Everything, done and said in the darkness, will be exposed in the light. Every wrong shall be righted.

"Therefore whatever you have said in the dark shall be heard in the light, and what you have whispered in private rooms shall be proclaimed on the housetops" Luke 12:3

"Whoever sows injustice will reap calamity, and the rod of his fury will fail." Proverbs 22:8

In 2018, I found my eyes glued to my television screen once again; but this time, it's not the faces of determined women I'm watching. It's the faces of determined children. Thousands of children throughout America "marching for their lives." My heart leaps from my chest into my throat. God's most precious gift had taken their lives out of our hands and placed it into their own because they no longer trusted us adults to protect them.

It was only after our children took their lives into their own hands that we, their "supposed" protectors and defenders, finally took "serious note" of their plight, only then did we adults, parents, and leaders "seriously" challenge the social and political status quo regarding firearms. Only then did we acknowledge the for-profit, widespread abuse of the Second Amendment. Similarly, it was only after our children went on strike over climate change, rose up in defiance, and declared, "We're fighting for our lives" that we adults seriously considered the environmental death sentence unleashed upon the Earth, generation after generation. Only then did we adults openly acknowledge our thoughtlessness, take individual responsibility for the part we each played and continue to play in the pollution, contamination, depletion, and desolation of our children's natural resources, their God-ordained environmental inheritance—a birthright promised and confirmed throughout the Word of God. From the poorest of us to the richest of us, we have conjointly violated, raped, and abused the Earth's natural resources and in so doing violated, abused, and raped our environmental inheritance and the inheritance of future generations. As we were entrusted to Earth, the Earth was entrusted to us. At present Earth is the only trustee endeavoring to fulfill its purpose-created responsibility. The earth has been crying out for decades, hoping to get our attention. Hurricanes, typhoons, cyclones, tornadoes, volcanic eruptions, avalanches, earthquakes, snow squalls, tsunamis, mudslides, melting ice caps, floods, but we refused to listen; we refused to see; we didn't care. We renounced our duty of care; our inherent obligation to protect the Sanctity of Earth, created by God; for the lies, false promises, and pleasures of a world fabricated by man. Now, our children are crying out, hoping to get our attention, begging us to stop destroying their inheritance. Will we listen? Will we seriously listen?

Why are our children marching for their lives? Why are our children fighting for their lives? Isn't that our job as parents, protectors, guardians, and caregivers? Somewhere along the way, we lost sight of our life purpose and therein lost sight of ourselves and our children. Somewhere along the way, we swapped human life for money and creature comforts. Somewhere along the way, we exchanged need for greed. Somewhere along the way, we exchanged responsibility for irresponsibility and accountability for unaccountability. Somewhere along the way, the wealthy, well-known, popular, and influential *few*, started believing they're more deserving than the middle-class, poor, less-known, less-popular "seemingly" uninfluential *many! Not!*

The few, seated in high places, are seated there because we, the many, placed him/her there. Whether we placed him/her in those high places as registered voters or consumers doesn't matter. What matters is our trust and our laws have been broken and will continue to be broken until "we the many" change our way of thinking and start seeing ourselves through the honest eyes of the spirit, rather than the lying eyes of the flesh. Only then will "we the many" reclaim the power and authority we so foolishly threw away. *United* we are many! *United* we are powerful! *United* we have authority! *United* we hold ourselves accountable! We are, equality! We are, liberty! We are justice! Saved by grace! Endowed with God's unmerited favor! *United* we are, change!

We the people are the United States of America; the United States of America is we the people. We are *one* and the *same*! Somewhere along the way, the elected, wealthy, popular, and influential *few* appear to have forgotten that! It is up to us "we the *many*" to remind them how they got where they are! No one gets anywhere in this world without the help of others! We the many are the voters! We the many are the consumers! There is no rich, famous, privileged, silver-spoon fed or self-made man or woman; without we the many! When we the many don't exercise our right to vote, we do ourselves and others a disservice. How? When we don't vote, we inadvertently vote for the very person or thing we're against. There's no such thing as "I didn't like any of the candidates so I'm not voting for anyone." Believe me when I say whether we actually vote or not, we vote!

When we spend selfishly, without regard, extravagantly, or inconsiderably thinking only of ourselves; when we drive our vehicles excessively; when we litter and pollute; when we support corporations that litter and pollute; when we continue to purchase environmentally unsafe products; when we don't hold government responsible for providing corporations with environmental loopholes; when we choose unrighteous convenience over righteous inconvenience, we disregard our Lord, our children, ourselves, one another, and the planet.

"Men will be lovers of self, lovers of money, boastful, haughty, idolaters, unthankful and unholy. Pride goes before destruction; a haughty

spirit before a fall. Things spoken in darkness shall be brought into the light; hidden things will be revealed. Lie succumbs to truth; arrogance will be put to shame. The arrogant will stumble and fall; no one will help them up; they will be removed from high places; their titles and glory stripped away." Timothy 3:2, Proverbs 16:18, Luke 12:3

Oftentimes, it's the incomprehensible, destructive things that prove to be most beneficial, constitute healing, and initiate change. Though incomprehensible, destructive things inflicted cannot be undone, God—knowing these incomprehensible, destructive things would come to pass—planted His sufficient grace in our hearts and in the land. Human life and the life of the planet—disrupted by forces beyond their/its control—God will restore, renew, and replenish. When great evil is loosed upon God's creation—man, woman, child, and land—a greater good is loosed in hot pursuit!

Jesus fights for us twenty-four hours a day, seven days a week; but because we often find ourselves lacking and wanting; we've grown lazy. Lazy regarding God, our children, ourselves, one another, our environment, and our country. Because of our lazy indifference, our children cry out in desperation. Our lives are pledged by trials and tribulations. We can't look past the color of our skin long enough to see ourselves in one another. The planet dies more each day for the sake of greed and human convenience.

Because of our lazy indifference, the once-solid foundation of America cracks and crumbles. For the sake of prejudice, unrighteousness, and greed, we fall short of the laws and decrees of both God and man. God's laws and decrees according to His eternal purpose. The Founding Fathers' laws, decrees, and mandates, in accordance to this…

Permeable to the United State Constitution

> We the people of the United States, in order to form a more perfect union, establish justice, insure domestic tranquility, provide for the common defense, promote the general welfare, and secure the blessings of liberty to ourselves

and our posterity, do ordain and establish this Constitution for the United States of America.

And this…

The Declaration of Independence

We hold these truths to be self-evident, that all men are created equal, that they are endowed by their Creator with certain unalienable rights, that among these are Life, Liberty, and the Pursuit of Happiness.

America is a promised of sanctuary to all mankind. When we disavow that promise, we disavow our brothers and sisters. When we disavow our brothers and sisters, we disavow ourselves. When we disavow ourselves, we disavow our purpose.

"Where there is no guidance, a people falls, but in an abundance of counselors there is safety." Proverbs 11:14

God purposed us individually and conjointly. Our individual purpose is instrumental to our collective purpose. Our collective purpose is instrumental to God's eternal purpose.

"Let there be no division between us, that we be united in the same mind and conviction. That we have sympathy, brotherly love, a tender heart, and a humble mind." 1 Peter 3:8

Unity plants substance and grows abundance; division sows greed and sprouts lack. United we stand, divided we fall! We are counsels graced to guide one another. When we help one another, God helps us realize our individual purpose. When we realize our individual purpose, we strive toward our collective purpose. When we strive toward our collective purpose, we discern God's eternal purpose.

Satan wants us to hate because of…

God wants us to love in spite of…

Reflections of Israel

When I look at President Trump, I see King Saul. When I look at America, I see the nation of Israel. I see mirroring leaders and mirroring nations. I see Israel's past in America's present. I see then and now simultaneously.

The Israelites were God's chosen people; the Prophet Samuel was their leader, but that all changed when the elders of Israel went to Samuel's home, told him he was too old to be their leader, pointed out how sinful his sons were, and demanded he appoint them a king to judge them like the other nations. Though the elders' demands upset Samuel, he delivers their demands to God, who in turn, instructs Samuel to give the people what they want. God tells Samuel not only had the nation of Israel rejected him as their leader; they had rejected Him as their King.

God knows Samuel made some serious mistakes as a leader. He also knows Samuel's sons are wicked, greedy and disrespectful. He also knows Samuel and his sons aren't Israel's primary problem; Israel's primary problem is Israel. God tells Samuel Israel hasn't been right since He freed them from Egypt, that since that day they had forsaken Him and served other gods. Rejecting Samuel was merely par for the course. When the Nation of Isreal demanded a king they told God they no longer needed or wanted him.

God instructed Samuel to warn Israel regarding the king they were choosing to reign over them, that he will take their belongings, sons, and daughters, produce, servants, and flock. He will be a tyrant. He will require a tenth of their goods, setting himself up as equal to God. Instead of serving Him, they will become slaves to their new king. But, the Israelites weren't having it; their minds were made up;

they wanted nothing more to do with God or Samuel. They wanted a new leader and a new king, a human king; they wanted to be like other nations; under the rule of man—not God. In time the Nation of Isreal will do exactly as God predicted.

God fought Israel's battles. He raised her above other nations. She was not oppressed, as some nations were. She was not poor, as some nations were. She did not want as some nations did. But having God champion her battles, being free, rich, and wanting for nothing wasn't enough for the people of Israel; they wanted to be like everybody else. And so, God allowed what the nation of Israel; His chosen people chose. And Samuel anointed King Saul, Israel's first "human king."

Some believe God never wanted Israel to have a king; I believe differently. I believe God promised kingship to the patriarchs/the father and/or ruler of a family or tribe; when He told Abraham He would make him exceedingly fruitful, make him into nations, and kings would come from him. This presupposes God wanted Israel to have a king. It also presupposes He wanted Israel to have a good and just king. A king, deserving of His chosen people."

I believe Israel was always destined to have a king, just not the king she chose. God desired only the best for His chosen people; His desire included the best king. What God desired in a king would take time, the nation of Israel had proven time and time again, they were an inpatient people. God wanted to give His chosen people His best, but His chosen people no longer wanted His best; they no longer wanted Him. I say this because the nation of Israel, after all God's warnings, still chose the tyrannical leadership of King Saul over the goodness of God, the King of kings. They chose the created being over the Creator; they chose to return to the oppressive, filth, muck, and mire from whence they came. They were proud, ignorant, and arrogant. They thought they could have their cake and eat it too. They thought they could have what God had to give as well as what the world "seemingly" had to offer. They thought wrong!

Shortly after becoming Isreal'new king; Saul does exactly what God warned he would do. He abuses and rapes Israel, destroys her stellar reputation throughout the nations, takes away everything God gave her, and enslaves her. Soon after, the Nation of Israel does exactly what God said she'd do. The people realize they made a horrible mistake and cry out to God. In turn, God does exactly as He said He would—He does not answer. When God saved the Israelites from slavery in Egypt, the Mosaic covenant was established between God and the nation of Israel. Israel broke her covenant with God when the people chose the callousness and greed of King Saul over the glory of God.

The nation of Isreal had everything a country could ever hope for—freedoms and riches other nations only dream of. But somewhere along the way, Isreal's desire to be like other nations took precedence over being God's chosen nation. When I look at President Trump, I see the greed, arrogance, bias, and maliciousness of King Saul. I believe King Saul had to have been biased to enslave the Israel nation. I believe he had to have been greedy to have taken Isreal's possessions for himself. I believe he had to have been arrogant to demand a tenth "tithe" of Isreal's goods, thereby setting himself up as equal to God.

Like President Trump, King Saul never hid who or what he was; like King Saul, President Trump warned America time and time again what kind of man he was, as God warned Isreal time and time again regarding king Saul's character; as Mr. Trump warned America time and time again regarding his character; as Isreal responded so to responded America. "That's okay, we just want a king. We just want to be like every other nation. We don't care what you did. We don't care what you're doing. We don't care what you're going to do to us. We don't care what you're going to take from us. We don't care what you're going to do to and take from others to manipulate us into thinking you actually care about us. We don't care if you never change, just tell us you're going to give us what we want: hurt the government the way the government hurt us. No need for you to change. We accept you as you are."

I imagine Mr. Trump must have thought to himself, *Alrighty then, if you don't care what I do, why should I? Let's get this party started.*

When I look at President Trump, I see loathing, gloating, and satisfaction. When I look at the world, I see powerful, envious nations plotting and anticipating America's ruination. I see less powerful admiring nations fearing what happens if America falls. I hear whisperings of America's downfall at home and abroad. I see enemies within and without. I hear the anguished cries of the Israelites, once they realized their horrific mistake, spilling from the mouths of the American people. I see a tyrant hell-bent on establishing his presidential legacy of chaos regardless of the cost, human or otherwise. I see nations that once admired America backing away. I see the same arrogant, prideful, self-indulgent, greedy, indifferent, ungrateful "it's all about me, the hell with everyone and everything" spirit that led to Israel's downfall courting America.

I say these things because of the inhumane treatment currently exhibited toward certain American citizens, residents, visitors, and foreigners. I say these things because like Isreal, somewhere along the way, America lost her way. I say these things because like Isreal, God freed America from the chains of slavery; freed her from the filth, muck, and mire of corruption and oppression, placed her atop a high hill and made her a nation above nations only for her to now entertain thoughts of the filth, muck, mire, corruption, and oppression from whence she came. Who does that? I'll tell you who does that. Isreal did it; America is running a close second.

Though I am compelled to speak out against the unrighteousness of President Trump, I do not take personal offense against him; he's a momentary affliction. I take personal offense against us; Mr. Trump may have voted for himself, but he didn't put himself in the White House, we the people did that. His presidency isn't on him; it's on us. When we put that checkmark next to his name. We told God, the American nation, and every nation on earth.

"We want to be like the other nations! We don't want a president! We want a dictator! We want a racist! We want a divider, separator, a conqueror. We want an instigator, liar, and thief! We want a womanizer and a manipulator! We want a bully! We want unrighteousness! We want a president who will take away our freedoms, liberties, and rights! We want a president who says one thing, does another, and denies ever having said anything!"

What does God say? He says the same thing He said regarding the Israelites, "Give the people what they want."

I do not fault Mr. Trump for the troubling situation we the American people find ourselves in. Why? Because just like Samuel warned the Israelites about the king, Mr. Trump warned us about himself; and just like the Israelites didn't heed Samuels's warning, we didn't heed Mr. Trump's warning. The Israelites told the king, do what you think best; we won't question you. We told Mr. Trump, do what you think best; we won't question you, and he did.

The hateful things we've thought about one another can't be "unthought." The awful things we've done to one another can't be undone. The horrible things we've said about one another, can't be unsaid. The worse thing we can do to ourselves and others is to hold on to things that can't be undone or unsaid. The best thing we can for one another when it comes to unchangeable things is repent; sincerely ask one another's forgiveness, and move on. If some of us are unwilling to forgive, we shake the dust from our feet, and keep it moving. Yesterday or yesteryear, the past is dead and gone. Today is the only day that matters! Where we go from here is the only thing that matters. How we treat and speak to one another moving forward is the only thing that matters. Can we love one another enough, can we forgive one another enough to *want* to change?

God's Favor

Despite her tragic history, God favored America, set her atop a high hill, made her a shining nation, a guiding light, a refuge of help, and hope for those in need. For us to stand idly by as she's stripped of her majesty and dignity, for us to look but refuse to see the terrified faces, hear but not heed the agonizing cries of our brothers and sisters of color is an affront to God. I spent my entire childhood watching those who could have done something, do nothing, those who could have said something, say nothing! Silent witnesses who deemed creature comforts more valuable than the life of a child! How much is a human life worth? God says we're priceless, yet we treat one another as if we're worthless.

There will soon come a day when our malicious intent and lack of regret demand retribution. Today may not be the day, tomorrow may not be the day, it might not be next week, next year, or even be in our lifetime, but it will come. When that day arrives, those who come after us, those who had nothing to do with the choices we're currently making will be held accountable! Our misdeeds, our bad choices, our ill intentions, our ill-spoken words will be brought to bear upon our children and generations to come; what brings us pleasure now; will bring them misery later. We're spiritually bankrupting ourselves, our children, and our nation. For what? Creature comforts, material crap, crap that will still be here after we're dead! Are we so angry, so fed up, we've become numb, deaf, and blind? Numb to the pain we're inflicting. Deaf to the anguished cries of our brothers and sisters. Blind to the lives we're unraveling. Numb, deaf, and blind to the inhumane precedent we're setting? Are we so consumed with want; we have no regard for the needs of others? Are we so *"me-consumed"* there is no room for *"we"*? Have *"we"* become one another's collateral damage?

Is it our intent to do to future generations what we "think" was done to us? Is this the American legacy we want to leave future generations? A legacy of degradation, indifference, prejudice, selfishness, covetousness, and greed. My biological father bequeathed me a legacy of worthlessness; my Heavenly Father God bequeaths me a legacy of pricelessnes. When I gave up on myself; God stood fast. When I hated myself, He loved me all the more. When I said I was unworthy, He said I was deserving. When I wanted to die, He said, *"You will live and not die."*

Evil is gathering up the worse parts of us; covertness, greed, indifference, prejudice, jealousy, hate; pride. And with them, he's spinning an inescapable web. A web of confusion and despair. A webbed prison for our children, grandchildren, and great-grandchildren. A web without hope or a future. But God has other plans; united we can expedite those plans. United we can protect our children, grandchildren, great-grandchildren, and the generations to come. We have to step up, brothers and sisters, as a nation and a people. We the people, we God's people must step up, speak out, and reaffirm our covenant with God. The United States of America must do what God favored her to do,

The colossal, neoclassical sculptured crowned woman that has stood on Liberty Island in New York Harbor since June 1885, with a raised torch in her right hand and the engraved adoption date "July 4, 1776," of the Declaration of Independence in her left hand, is a staunch reminder of the irrevocable words engraved upon her base. Promised words we the American people swore to uphold ad live by. A promise for all people, not some people! A promise for all time! Not part-time!

"Give me your tired, your poor, Your huddled masses yearning to breathe free, The wretched refuse of your teeming shore. Send these, the homeless, tempest-tossed to me, I lift my lamp beside the golden door!"

We are America! We are God's refuge! We are called to press on! For such a time as this! The Declaration of Independence has not changed since its conception. Its words ring just as true, loud, and free today as they did on July 4, 1776. "We hold these truths to be self-evident, that all men are created equal, that they are endowed by their *Creator* with certain Unalienable Rights, that among these are Life, Liberty and the Pursuit of Happiness."

All people! Not some people!

Unalienable rights, life, liberty, and the pursuit of happiness. Rights endowed by our Creator. Rights Christ Jesus came to Earth, suffered, and died for. Rights declared by our Founding Fathers that All men are created equal. Rights our servicemen and women put their lives on the line for time and time again. Who are we the people for whom these unalienable rights were established to declare some of us more deserving and others of us? What God endows; Christ guarantees. What God the Father endows and His Son guarantees—man cannot rescind.

When I was a girl, the stepfather stripped away my unalienable rights. He shamed me, humiliated me, degraded me, and broke me into pieces. Confident he had ruined me that I would never be of any good to anyone or anything, he threw me away. He died satisfied; satisfied he left me with nothing to pass on but brokenness; satisfied I would wreck my children before they had a chance to live; satisfied my children would build on my brokenness and thereby become broken; satisfied his legacy of brokenness would live on long after his death.

The stepfather chose me, his broken legacy, physical evidence of his life on Earth, his broken legacy to be continued and remembered generation after generation. Recalling who I was, where I was, the darkness, pain, and shame, I cannot help but cry, but not for myself. It took years for me to cry out for help, but once I did the Way came straight away and got me. He gathered up my broken pieces. Led me out of the darkness; into His light and restored me. Through Him, I found my way; I found my God-given purpose. *"I cry out to God Most High, to God who fulfills His purpose for me."* Psalm 57:2 I cry for those without a voice, those who have been silenced, those bound and chained in darkness—amid humanlight. I cry for know-ing-closed-shut-eyes and knowing-closed-tight-mouths. I pray silent witnesses to be silent no longer! I cry for those imprisoned in this present darkness, those being introduced to the darkness, those reentering the darkness, and those clinging to the darkness because the darkness is the only thing they know. I cry for those waiting and hoping to be rescued from the darkness, waiting to be taken from the arms of their oppressor. I cry for those who die in the darkness because we the people, we God's people, we God's light refuse to shine!

Just as my biological father's disregard for me caused evil to turn and take closer notice of me, our disregard as a nation has caused evil to turn and take closer notice of us. Evil has always hated America. America reminds him of Job; no matter what he takes from her, no matter what he does to her, she survives and thrives. But unlike Job, America had a horrific past. No one knows this better than Satan. He orchestrated and applauded the slaughter of the Indian/Native American Nation, strategized and danced amid the chained, broken, beaten, raped bodies imprisoned inside the bulging bellies of slave ships. Yet despite America's wickedness, God showed her the same favor as Job who did no wrong.

Evil watched America rise from the stench of filth, death, and decay into glory. He watched God establish her a nation above nations. He knew America was protected; just as he knew Job was protected. He knew her Constitution, Declaration of Independence, and Bill of Rights. He knew no matter how much damage he did, she would prevail. Because Satan knew these things regarding America, he set his sights on third-world countries; he unleashed unimaginable horrors upon them knowing America would come to their defense, but he didn't care. Something was better than nothing. If he couldn't have America, he would take what he could have, even if only for a short while.

But things are different now. America's light isn't nearly as bright, her shores are no longer welcoming, and she's far less glorious these days. America has placed herself back within evil's reach. What evil thought was beyond his reach is now within his grasp. The super power evil thought too strong and united to fail is failing. The endless, selfless prayers of the righteous that held evil in check for hundreds of years have become complacent, weak, self-serving, shallow, and whiny. Evil is crossing the thresholds of sanctuaries, churches, temples, synagogues, and mosques, entering homes he was never allowed to enter but now enters freely because of insincere prayer.

Evil comes for all of us sooner or later, some of us sooner than others. But as surely as day becomes night, and night becomes day, evil eventually comes for us all; no one's immune. Evil relishes our arrogance, cheers, and cultivates the person many of us refuse to believe we are; sinners saved by grace. The fact that some of us actually believe there isn't a higher power watching over us. That this life is all there is. That once we're gone, we're gone. Is mind-boggling. Evil doesn't know our hearts. It doesn't know what we're thinking; it doesn't know our bad or our good until we expose it. So it waits patiently, waits for us to show it. How to destroy us. How does evil know we'll eventually show it how to destroy us? It knows because we're sinners, and sin refuses to stay hidden.

The stepfather endeared himself to the bad, the good, and the supposed good. He went along with whomever/whatever people said they were. But he knew their truth; he knew their truth because he recognized himself in them. Their expressions, words, and actions told him everything he needed to know; what he needed to lie about; and what he needed to promise. He walked away from every encounter knowing exactly what his supporters/prey needed to believe and wanted to hear. They needed to believe he had their best interest at heart. They needed him to pretend to tell them the truth. They needed him to pretend he cared. They needed him to convince them; it's okay to be indifferent, selfish, and greedy. They needed him to tell them it's okay to choose, dead material things over the life of a child. In exchange for me; the stepfather gave his supporters/prey permission not to feel guilt or shame. Permission not to care. Permission to choose death over life.

The stepfather promised fearful, desperate, discontented, disappointed, angry people who had nothing, more nothing disguised as something, and they gobbled it up no questions asked. He told them lie after lie, promised them more and more stuff, stuff many of them didn't want and others thought was beneath them but didn't want anyone else to have. The more lies he told, the more promise he made; the more his prey/supporters excused and defended him. Why? Because varying life conditions and situations often dictate convenient lies and false promises are easier to accept than inconvenient truths.

My Immediate Concern

What becomes of us if we continue swapping inconvenient truths for convenient lies and false promises? What becomes of us if we keep choosing creature comforts over human life? If the life we're living is preparation for eternal life, what will eternal life look like based on our present-day preparations?

Mr. Trump says he wants to build a wall to keep Americans safe and keep undesirables out. What he calls protection, I call crap disguised as crap! None of us have the authority to declare some of us more deserving than others of us. Jesus says we are to love one another as He loves us. At *no* time does He say only love those who look like you, think like you, love like you, or believe as you believe. It is written, though none of us are worthy, all of us are deserving; that all have sinned and fall short of the glory of God. Who are we, the created, to say differently?

God spoke each of us into existence. He declared us equals and granted each of us the same rights, liberties, and freedoms. He declared none greater than others. Mr. Trump is the "current" president of America. As there were presidents before him, there will be presidents after him. This is the way of man—he comes; he goes. God is Creator, Maker, Designer, and Author of all things. There was no other before Him; there shall be no other after Him. He is the Truth, the Life, and the Way. He created the Earth. He entrusted the Earth to the whole of mankind. He bestowed a small portion of the Earth to the nation currently known as the United States of America. He placed His favor upon her and appointed her leaders and citizens, ambassadors of solidarity, givers of hope, open hearts, welcoming shores, and open arms.

What happens to God's favor when we the people, His ambassadors of solidarity, givers of hope, open hearts, welcoming shores, and open arms stop doing what we were entrusted, enriched, and empowered to do? What happens to God's favor when our only concern is ourselves? What happens to God's favor when we allow ourselves to be walled in, separated, and divided from those we were entrusted, enriched, and empowered to help? What happens to God's favor when we choose the created over the Creator? What happens to God's favor when we prefer convenient lies and false promises to inconvenient truths? What happens to God's favor when we give way to apathy, desperation, greed, and fear rather than stand and fight the good fight?

"No one can serve two masters: Either he will hate the one and love the other, or he will be devoted to the one and despise the other. We cannot serve both God and money." Matthew 6:28

That being said, we cannot serve both God the Creator and Mr. Trump the created.

When I envision a walled-in America, I see dark skies and falling ash. She no longer sits atop a high hill. She no longer shines. She no longer constitutes hope, help, or a future. Her welcoming shores, vanquished by muck, and mire. Her glory, an obscure distant memory. Her compassion, scattered to the four winds. Her majesty soiled, left withering by the wayside. Once extraordinary now less than ordinary; future generations destined to suffer the consequences of past generations. The old, weary, and dying remember America's strength, power, glory, and compassion; they speak of her in whispers for fear of being overheard. They whisper of God's abundant favor. How He lifted America from blood, ash, and bone and placed her a magnificent sight to behold atop a high hill high above other nations. Yet the more God favored America, the more satisfied and proud she became. And like Isreal, she forgot Him. Race rebelled against race. Men rebelled against women. Daughters rebelled against mothers. Sons rebelled against fathers. Cities rebelled against cities. States rebelled against states. Citizens rebelled against leaders. Leaders rebelled against citizens. The world watches in horror and disbelief as the nation God favored, rose from death and decay, returns to from whence she came. Those America once fed, sheltered, and protected are deported and turned away. Enemies, foreign and domestic, rejoice. Look! See what has become of America! And evil beams with delight as he dances amid the devastation he loosed upon the nation God once favored. The United States of America.'

God watches us with a heavy heart. The nation He rose up from the ashes has forgotten Him in lieu of themselves, forfeiting His favor for the convenient lies and false promises of man. God does not extend favor to rescind it; He does not make promises to break them. Our words and actions determine what God does and/ or doesn't do. God will never leave or forsake us. Can we say the same thing about ourselves regarding Him? Every time we leave and forsake one another, we leave and forsake God. Everything we say and do to one another, we do and say to God first.

When I look at Mr. Trump, I see my childhood in full bloom on a global scale. I see prison walls manned by a single guard holding all the keys, a guard who somehow managed to convince not all of us but enough of us that he was the best thing that ever happened to us that we should not only turn our backs on those in need but have them pay for a wall to keep them out, imprisoning ourselves in the process. Mr. Trump says "his border wall" will be a barrier of protection for Americans. I say it will be an American prison built by Americans to imprison Americans—physical evidence of our disregard. Mr. Trump's ultimate salute to himself, a wall statue to President Trump from Salesman Trump, a wall-legacy of *inhumanity*! Is this how we want future generations to see us?

President Trump appears to be under the misconception that America belongs to him, that he can do whatever he wants whenever he wants. America doesn't belong to man nor woman; she belongs to her Creator. Allowing President Trump to build "his wall" on God's property doesn't benefit anyone other than President Trump. Truth be told, it won't even benefit him; he just hasn't realized it yet. Like so many of us, he looks but doesn't see; hears but doesn't listen. The question is, how many of us are willing to continue following him on this fraudulent, fruitless journey? How many of us are willing to lose God's favor for President Trump's convenient lies and false promises? We can't possibly think America got where she is because of us, can we? God says His children perish for lack of knowledge.

Question: What does "We perish for lack of knowledge" say about us? Well, considering our current state of affairs, I'd say we lack the compassion to care about others more than ourselves. That we value money and creature comforts more than human life. That we prefer the sinking sands of convenient lies and false promises over the heavy bricks of inconvenient truths.

Many of us try to justify our actions by saying we chose the "lesser evil." Newsflash! There's no such thing as a lesser evil! Evil can't be measured like a cup of sugar! It can't be less than what it is. Even if it were capable of subtracting from itself, it wouldn't; it exists to destroy. It's always adding, always growing, always thriving in accordance with our words, misdeeds, and bad choices. Evil has one purpose; that purpose is to serve itself, and the only way to do that is via us. Evil is sitting at the dinner table; every country before America was an appetizer. America is the main course; she's the meal evil constantly craves; the insatiable hunger he developed in 1492; when Christopher Columbus set sail. And America was subsequently stolen; from her rightful inhabitants.

Nothing good can come from what we're doing and allowing. The America I'm seeing goes against everything she was raised up to be. It's like watching one of my children go off the rails after years of care, prayer, love, and sacrifice. One minute everything is right as rain; the next you find yourself standing in the middle of a monsoon.

If we allow Mr. Trump to build his wall, we allow him to declare to the world his wall is the United States of America! His wall is we the people. I look at Mr. Trump and I see what happens when choices are made based on prejudice, fear, greed, disappointment, lack, and the need to get even. I see what happens when we take our freedoms, liberties, and rights for granted. I see what happens when good people do nothing. What happens when we assume? What happens when we allow power and authority to go unchecked? What happens when we elect arrogance, prejudice, apathy, greed, and self-ishness to the highest seat in the land out of spite?

Fear builds walls. Cowardice builds walls. Arrogance builds walls. Unacceptance builds walls. Hatred builds walls. Prejudice builds walls. Apathy builds walls. Lack of empathy builds walls. Sexism builds walls. We are *not* those things! We are we the children of God, brothers and sisters of Christ, and temples of the Holy Spirit. President Trump is a salesman; we're his commission, the biggest sale he ever made in his life. He can't collect that commission without decommissioning us! We the people are his crowning glory, the center stone in his crown of chaos! But that's not all President Trump intends us to be. If we build his wall, we give him his throne. If we give him his throne, we become his footstool.

When I look at President Trump, I see a man living in the present longing for the past. A man who wants the luxuries and freedoms of the present but longs for past prejudices, freedom belonging only to the chosen. I see past sufferings. I see whips, ropes, and chains, dividers, wreckers and destroyers, hoarders and takers. When he speaks I hear self-proclaimed-superiority, slavery, rape, murder, disregard, hate, and greed; America's past laughing and rejoicing "I'm still here." When I listen, I hear inequality, sorrow, despair, agony, heartache, and pain; America's present crying in disbelief.

Everything the world places beyond our reach, God places within our grasps. The world declares some of us undeserving, unworthy of its offerings. Yet God declares none of us are worthy, but all of us are deserving of all He has to offer. Isn't it interesting that the Creator and Owner of everything disagrees with the world? Everything the world offers we can acquire by way of Christ. Yet we can't acquire anything God offers by way of the world. What we need to start asking ourselves is what we're doing or not doing, saying or not saying that's blocking our prayer request.

"If we ask it will be given to us. If we knock the door will be open unto us. If we seek we will find." Matthew 7:7

Being a Christian or not being a Christian doesn't determine God's blessings. Our intent, the unseen, unspoken things, the secrets of the heart determine whether God allows or disallows. God isn't going to bless us to do harm to ourselves and/or others. He's going to do whatever it takes to protect us from the enemy, even if that enemy is us.

God created us to invest in one another, to increase one another. We are one another's profit. We are one another's loss. We can't increase one another without increasing ourselves. We can't decrease one another without decreasing ourselves. Why? Because that's how God designed us. *"Do unto others as you would have them do unto you."* Matthew 7:12 We profit as a whole; we lose as a whole. We are the whole of one another. When a threat rises against one of us, it rises against the whole of us! It is expected when there is a recognized threat against one of us, we will rise up as a whole in defense of the one. Though we are one, we are many. We fight for the whole of who we are. We fight for we the people. We fight for the whole of humanity. We don't let up! We don't give up! We don't grow weary! We don't grow faint! We fight as a whole until the threat to the one is eliminated!

Though we appear at an impasse, my hope resides in us as a people. My hope resides in knowing we have a choice. My hope resides in believing when the time comes, we will choose correctly. My solace resides in knowing we are the men and women God authored, designed, and created us to be—fearless, loving, kind, and just. My confidence resides in knowing we are not the fearful men and women we've been deceived into "thinking" we should be if we're to survive the likes of this world.

It's time we stopped running around like chickens with our heads cut off, looking for "the" answer. The answer is what it has been since before the beginning. The answer is *love*! Love reassures we're more than the things we've said; we're more than the things we've done. No matter how far we fall, we never fall too far to love. None are worthy; all are deserving. Love will never leave or forsake us. Love is patient and kind. It does not envy or boast. It is not arrogant or rude. It does not insist on its own way; it is not irritable or resentful; it does not rejoice at wrongdoing but rejoices with the truth. It keeps no record of wrongs. Love bears all things, believes all things, hopes all things, endures all things. "Love never dies. Inspired speech will be over some day; praying in tongues will end; understanding will rea*ch it*s limit. We know only a portion of the truth, and what we say about God is always incomplete. But when the Complete arrives, our incompletes will be canceled." 1 Corinthians 13:8-10 *Love never dies! Love never ends!*

With so much abounding love, forgiveness, grace, and mercy, how can we not love one another? How can we not forgive one another? How can we not show one another grace and mercy? This isn't about how far we've fallen; it's about how quickly we get up, how quickly we help one another up. We the people will rise stronger and mightier once we the people realize though we are many; we are One United People! How do I know this? I know this because united in love trumps divided in hate; united by faith trumps divided by fear; united in generosity trumps divided in greed; united in grace and mercy trumps divided in thoughtlessness and cruelty. United by good trumps divided by evil. United in righteousness trumps divided in unrighteousness. My disconcerting truth, Mr. Trump wasn't God preferred; he was God allowed. Based on the choices we made.

At some point in my life, I don't know when I became my prison, and my guard. I held the keys to my freedom but I didn't set myself free. The men who imprisoned me as a child were dead and gone. The men who imprisoned me once I became a woman were no longer a part of my life, yet I was still a prisoner. I didn't know how to free myself. Not to mention; I had no idea what it meant to be free. God freed me; God taught me the way I should go. God created me with you in mind. He created you with me in mind. When I look at you, I see me. I love us! I love we the people. We are God's people; we are His children. We are so much more than we can imagine; so much more than we give ourselves, and one another credit for. I don't want what happened to me as a child to happen to us as a people.

I don't want us to become prisoners of ourselves within ourselves. I don't want us to alienate ourselves from ourselves.

"Therefore what God has joined together, let man not separate." Mark 10:9

We are one! God put us together for *good reason!* Let no man separate us from one another. Let no man separate us from our Father.

Should I look at someone and see skin color, gender, personal preference—pretty, ugly, skinny, fat, tall, short, well-dressed, ill-dressed? The problem isn't the person I'm looking at; the problem is me. Why? Because the only thing I should see when I look at someone is a child of God. My brother and/or sister.

We Can Do All Things

We are the sons and daughters of God; we are family. As our division is of our making and choosing, so too shall our reunification be of our making and choosing. But that reunification cannot happen; will not happen—until we stop pointing fingers and demeaning one another. Until we stop picking and choosing, and start loving, and forgiving, in spite of rather than because of. America isn't the largest country in the world, but it's the most powerful.

Why do you think that is? Why would God make the third-largest country in the world the most powerful country in the world? Why not the first-largest country, or even the second-largest country? Why the third?

I've always been fascinated by numbers, not mathematics; I hated math in school. I'm fascinated by the meaning of numbers; what they represent. Not what numbers represent according to man, but what they represent according to the Word of God—biblical numerology.

According to the Word of God, the number three is a big deal. Not only is it symbolic of the Father, the Son, and the Holy Spirit, it also represents divine wholeness, completeness, and perfection. It is a divine stamp of completion/approval on the subject. Remember when I told you a while back that grace and mercy are given, but God's favor is approved? Case and point: America was approved when she became one nation under God's indivisible. She was approved when she opened her shores to foreigners. She was approved when the United States Constitution was born and later adopted. She was approved when the Declaration of Independence was written and adopted. She was approved when the Bill of Rights was written, signed, and adopted. She was approved when the Human Rights Articles were written, established, and adopted. She was further approved when the Civil Rights Act was written, passed, and signed into law.

America was approved when she upheld the written promise of the Founding Fathers. Men who held themselves accountable—acknowledged and took responsibility for the human atrocities committed under their leadership and the leadership of those who came before them. These men gave their solemn promise, their stamp of approval to God and country—by way of their signatures—that the human atrocities committed in the past would never again take place on American soil. Yet, here we are, allowing past atrocities to spread anarchy and chaos throughout our present. Atrocities that want to lay waste to both present and future. We cannot defeat this evil divided! The number of our good far outweighs the number of our bad. We are the children of God. We are family! We must unite as a family. We must step out on faith as a family. We must trust and believe! If we do right by one another, God will do the rest! We are America's light! We are America's hope! Evil wants to drown America's hope, he wants to extinguish her flame before those needing sanctuary reach her shores.

Evil has walked the earth since God created the first man and woman, yet he has always been hesitant about unleashing his full vengeance upon America—he's no longer hesitant. He has unleashed all of his hate and filth upon the American people. When we voted wickedness into the oval office we told God we no longer needed Him; He was no longer our King. To regain what we lost we must take up our cross; we must retrieve and cloak ourselves in the Mantel of Sanctuary; we so foolishly discarded. We must resecure the rights, freedoms, and liberties we once held dear. We must reunite! One People Under God!—Indivisible! Evil can't destroy us without us! Love can't save us without us! Divided we are glass. United we are steel! Despite the wrongs, we've said. Despite the wrongs, we've done!—Grace and Mercy assure us every second of every day—We will NEVER fall too far for God to love!

Despite our hateful words and misdeeds, I stand resolute…

"For I am convinced that neither death nor life, neither angels nor demons, neither the present nor the future, nor any powers, neither height nor depth, nor anything else in all creation, will be able to separate us from the love of God that is in Christ Jesus our Lord." Romans 8:38–39

This planet upon which we reside is temporary; it will soon pass away. We are destined for a far greater place! We are destined for far greater things. Until that time, take comfort in knowing the kingdom of God resides in each of us. I believe in us. I believe together, there's *nothing* we cannot do.

We Are Our Matter of Choice

We are one another's matter of choice; we are our determining factors. Hence, there's no such thing as *"The only person I hurt was myself. He/she only hurt him/herself. "That has nothing to do with me." Your problem; not mine."* etcetera; etcetera. Like it or not we are related; brothers and sisters; Intentionally or unintentionally, everything we do or say as individuals affects us as a whole—in one way or another. Satan knows this! This is why he celebrates our willful disobedience, our self-imposed blindness, our deliberate deafness; disrespect, and indifference. He muddies our hearts, clouds our minds, seduces our eyes, and muffles our ears. He misdirects where and when we look; to whom/what we should turn a blind eye. He distorts what and how we hear; to whom/what we should turn a deaf ear. Centuries of misdirection and manipulation have persuaded evil, he knows us better than we know ourselves; persuaded him we are a defiant, selfish, greedy, predictable people. He [supposes] we will not see. We will not listen. We will not recognize God's still small voice. We will not heed the direction of the Holy Spirit. We will not confess Christ. We will not admit our ugly, inconvenient truth.

"It is not the color of our skin that divides, separates, robs, kills, and destroys us. It is the color of our character."

We are our greatest asset; we are our greatest liability. We are lenders, borrowers, profit and loss. We are mistakes made, lessons learned, lessons unlearned, lessons not learned, and lessons waiting to be learned. We are peacemakers; we are lawbreakers. We are givers; we are takers. We are promises made; we are promises broken. We are arbitrators; we are instigators. We are the judge; we are the jury. We are doctor; we are patient. We are flowers; we are weeds. We are brick walls; we are wrecking balls. We are hope; we are despair. We are the giants standing in our way; we are the slingshots and stones that bring those giants down. We are potholes causing one another to stumble and fall; we are asphalt filling those potholes. We are prison bars holding one another captive; we are master keys setting one another free. We are the problem; we are the solution. We are the best of us; we are the worst of us.

Nothing in the heavens nor upon the earth can make us choose one another. Who and what we choose is a matter of choice. Everything we do or say is a matter of choice. Everything we do not do or do not say is a matter of choice. We are far more than this human life we're living. We are better than the choices we're making for and against one another. We were designed to pick one another up when we fall, not kick one another when we're down. Fighting for right often generates uncertainty about what's to come. Defending wrong guarantees the certainty nothing will come. Good does not prevail because of evil; good prevails in spite of evil. Evil has not changed its MO (modus operandi) since the garden of Eden. It hasn't change because we haven't changed. If it ain't broke, don't fix it. Evil is counting on us to look the other way. Look but not see; hear but not listen. Evil is self-consuming us. Self-consumption doesn't leave room for anyone or anything else. Evil is not going to change. We have to change. We have to change for ourselves; we have to change for one another individually and collectively worldwide!

Only when we see as God sees. Only when we listen as God listens. Only when we love one another as Christ Jesus loves us will God open up the windows of heaven and pour down blessings we won't have room enough to receive until there is no more need. Only when we chose to see one another in ourselves, only when we choose to love one another above *all* else. Only then…

Final Thought

There are those of us who will view what I've written as religious hogwash, the illogical foolishness, misguided ramblings of an old woman. To those of us who feel this way, I ask the following. What if you're wrong? What if everything I've written is exactly as I've written? To those of us who think this way, I say it's okay. Jesus didn't die for us to agree with one another; He died that we might live and not die. Regardless of our belief or disbelief in Him, regardless of our opinion of one another, we were a gift to Jesus from His Father. Jesus knows everything there is to know about us. He knows what we know. He knows what we "think" we know. He knows what we don't know. He knows what we will come to know. He knows what we will never know. He knows how we think and why. He sees what we do. He listens when we speak. Some of the things we think, do, and say are soul-wrenching and spirit-clenching. Oftentimes, we can't even make sense of some of the stuff we think, do, and say. In steps, Jesus. He knows every part of us, intimately. He sees us in ways we can't begin to imagine. He takes all that He knows, every part of us, into His thoughtful consideration—the good, bad, and indifferent. He intercedes for us; He presents the best parts of us to His/our Father, daily. He knows we are *not* "always" the choices we make. He knows we're *not* "always" as we appear.

When Jesus took His last breath on Earth, He took it knowing some of us would be just, others of us unjust. He took our first and last breath with Him. He took it knowing He would be with us at our beginning and at our end. At the end of this place, when Earth ceases to exist, time will stand before its Maker and be stilled, that we might comtemplate all that we have said and done. This will be our final choice, not as a whole but as individuals. Sadly, even then, God's heart will break, for some of us will still not choose Him.

God is our first breath when physical life begins; He is our last breath when physical life ends. He is our countless breaths in-between. God is not an obligatory choice; He's a personal choice. At the end of this place, we stand before Him alone. But even then, His hope remains the same—that none should perish. He will fight for us until the very end. Yet though He fights for us, He cannot choose for us.

Christ paid the ultimate price, the only acceptable ransom—that we might live and not die. Whether we *choose* to use our free will for good or evil does not increase nor decrease the divine mandate Christ imposed upon Himself, on our behalf. A mandate of betrayal, heartache, torment, and suffering; death by crucifixion. A mandate of sacrifice! Unconditional, wholly, complete love! A love that promised to never leave or forsake us! Love notwithstanding! Regardless of what we did. Regardless of what we said. Regardless...

> Who is there to condemn us? For Christ Jesus, who died, and more than that was raised to life, is at the right hand of God—and He is interceding for us. (Romans 8:34)

Jesus went to the cross knowing He left Himself noway out. Knowing He would be betrayed and crucified by the very ones He came to save. Why! Why would He do such a thing? He Promised! Unconditional Love!

All Knowing

God witnessed the evolution of evil eons before evil realized what he was; before he fully comprehended the scope and magnitude of his immorality; before he became—evil personified. Knowing evil's inhuman intentions, God anchored lifesaving measures/provisions throughout human history to assist His children in times of need.

Steadfast love and forgiveness. Renewed grace and mercy. Resolute power and authority.

The moment God breathed life into the nostrils of man—from our physical beginning until our physical end; then, now, and beyond; that one breath spans space and time, generation after generation; breathing life into the nostrils and filling the lungs of mankind—the spirit of God; revealer of truth and purpose; distributor of spiritual gifts and heavenly insight; comforter, teacher, guide, and affirmation; who we are, what we are, why we are, when we began. Keeper of forgotten languages and hidden memories; unchanged and protected—since before there was time. That at the appointed time, when Satan comes to claim mankind as his own, we, God's children, might know our Father's voice above all other voices. That we, God's children, might *rightly* and *justly* interpret and execute God's one truth, amid Satan's countless lies. That we, God's children, might discern—lies shout to distract, shout to conceal; shout to overpower. That we, God's children, might discern—truth whispers to engage, whispers to reveal; whispers to empower. That we, God's children, might further discern our royal identity; that we are *not* ordinary! We are *extraordinary*! We are a peculiar people unto God.

In the beginning, one life-giving breath, from God, opened the nostrils and filled the lungs of the whole of humanity. Centuries later, here we stand! Here we live! Here we breathe! This present generation! *God's sons and daughters* brought to life inside the sanctum of the womb, *breathing* the same breath as Adam—in the beginning. How will we live the life God breathed into us? How will we honor the blood Christ shed for us? How will we adhere to the direction of the Holy Spirit within us? How?

> But there is a spirit in man: and the inspiration of the Almighty giveth them understanding. (Job 32:8)

Life

Life is free will/personal choice. Embracing our design, our sameness, is a personal choice. Rejecting our design, our sameness, is a personal choice. We choose to love one another. We choose to hate one another. Thing is, we cannot love one another without loving ourselves just as we cannot hate one another without hating ourselves. Simply put, no matter how fast we run, no matter how far we run, we cannot escape one another—we *are* one another.

Christ is the Way, the Truth, and the Life; our 24-hour Open-Door Policy to the Father. Though the Holy Spirit leads and guides 24/7; He cannot push us regarding the Way we should go; the Truth and the Life. He cannot pull us through Christ Open Door. We must walk through willingly. We must walk through freely. We must walk through, of our own accord. To be an insider in Christ is to be an outsider; in the world."

"Love not the world, neither the things that are in the world. If any man loves the world, the love of the Father is not in him. For all that is in the world, the lust of the flesh, and the lust of the eyes, and the pride of life, is not of the Father but is of the world. And the world passeth away, and the lust thereof: but he that doeth the will of God abideth forever." 1 John 2:15-17

My life truth: Life is a test of faith. Faith is a testament to life.

My concluding truth. We are not our mistakes; we are not the bad choices we've made. We are the sons and daughters of God almighty, God who bequeathed to us His only Begotten Son, Christ Jesus! Our do-over! Over and over and over. Seventy times seven. What are we going to do with the do-over God has bequeathed us, keeping in mind tomorrow is not promised?

> From one man God made every nation of men, that they should inhabit the whole earth; and he determined the times set for them and the exact places where they should live. God did this so that men would seek him and perhaps reach

out for him and find him, though he is not far from each one of us. (Acts 17:26)

I leave you with these words. There is no evil greater than God's prevailing good. There is no greater weapon than love. There is no greater comforter than love. When we finally come to the end of ourselves, God will be waiting. Death is inconsequential; it comes for us all. What matters most is this. When death arrives, in what state will it find us? A state of eternal life or a state of eternal death. What we did for self dies with us. What we did for others lives on.

The beginning

CPSIA information can be obtained
at www.ICGtesting.com
Printed in the USA
LVHW071619230322
713949LV00008B/1